B O R N for W O R S H I P

the best you can be in worship-arts ministry

conversations with Timothy J Miller

Born For Worship: The Best You Can Be In Worship-Arts Ministry

Details in some anecdotes and stories have been changed to protect the identities of the persons involved.

KDP ISBN 978-1-7967-5537-4

Printed in the United States of America
2019—First Edition

DEDICATION

To Jesus—it's all about You in the first place.

Thank you for choosing to share Yourself with us, for calling us to walk with You, for making it possible for us to be continually transformed as Your masterpiece. Enable us to reflect You better and better in unity, depth, impact, and love as we become the perfected Bride You envision.

ACKNOWLEDGMENTS

Many frontrunner worship pioneers helped shape my growth as a worshiper. I'd like to specifically acknowledge Glenn Kaiser, Pat Boone, MW Smith, Andy Parks, Don Potter, Dan Wilt, Paul Baloche, Chris Tomlin, and Darlene Zschech.

I'm incredibly thankful for my family! My kids Jonathan, Katie, Kristin, and Tabor—it's so exciting that all of you serve in worship-arts ministry (and Kristin for helping produce this book and all the other materials at Hearts In Tune WORSHIP)! My parents—your support and insight opened me to everything this book discusses. Special thanks to my sis Tina (in many ways you made this book possible) and bro Todd (your outside-of-worship-world-but-inside-of-ministry perspective was so insightful), and of course my wife Anita (how many times could I say invaluable?).

My Insight Team provided great encouragement while I finalized these pages. Thank you for your willingness to tell me plainly when I missed the mark, with special thanks to Jerry Hershberger and Mark Powers. Glenn Planck, your introspective lens and significant editing work proved indispensible, Courtney Abbott-Fogie, for your keen eye, and Sheri Gould, I so appreciate the way you sacrificially offered both support and helpful nudges along the way. You've all made this a much better book!

To everyone I've led and served with over the years—you helped me through the learning curve (sorry for that!). Know that our time together has been one of the great joys in my life.

A note from the author...

You know those moments when suddenly you realize you'll never be the same? You've become MORE. More capable, more strong, *more the you that God created you to be.*

How exciting!

That's what this book celebrates. And that's my prayer for you.

MORE!

For many people, though, experiencing a sense of *more* while serving is tough. People usually sense when they are *not* the best they can be.

That's why helping people experience such moments has become my focus for 3 decades in the worship-arts ministry trenches. I've learned so much by yearly pastoring over 100 musicians and technician. It's one of the greatest things that excites me about developing worship leaders. And even though I have about a dozen degrees and certifications under my belt, there's always more to discover. Besides, some of my best growth experiences have come from serving in small, mid-sized, and multi-site churches.

As a Ministry Coach, I write about leadership and worship, and help churches grow. I'm discovering that my best impact occurs while assisting people to experience their own greater impact. You could consider me to be your thinking partner or a growth catalyst.

If you understand the depth of my passion that you embrace all the Lord has for you in your worship-arts ministry role, it may surprise you that I've put off writing this book for years.

It's not that I don't write. I've written magazine articles, on-line helps, manuals, procedurals, assessments, and training materials. I've helped nearly a thousand businesses communicate better with clients. I've taught worship workshops, produced training conferences, coached hundreds of musicians and teams, and even written books for internationally known evangelists and speakers as a ghost writer.

But this content needed to wait and mature. Now I think the Lord is nudging and saying, "It's time."

So you hold in your hand something very dear to me—with the one goal that you can be effective in ministry and that you can help others do the same.

I can't take full credit for everything in this book. In addition to all those who have impacted my development over the years, I must thank my Insight Team. Their frank comments were peppered with encouragement. Their observations deepened what you discover within these pages and saved you from some material you wouldn't have wanted to read. One way I thanked them was to add individual thank-you's right in the context of the book. They earned it. I'm humbled and grateful for their investment in me and in you.

I'm also grateful to the Launch Team. Their willingness to help get the word out may be the reason you're reading this now.

So I'm excited to see the MORE that the Lord unfolds through this project. I'd love to hear your own stories of ministry and of the lessons you've paid so dearly to learn!

I invite you to contact me via my website, www.htworship.com, where you'll find my email addy, additional resources, links to Instagram, Facebook, and so on.

And if you find this content helpful, please help by letting others know!

Now I invite you to sit back and relax. Enjoy this read. Stop as you need to pause and introspect with the Lord. Consider this time as a conversation. I pray you'll find ideas that you can apply or share with someone else to increase their impact on this wild ride of serving the Lord through worship-arts ministry. Blessings!

CONTENTS

FIRST THINGS FIRST

1.0 BATS IN THE BELFRY

Did you ever experience a situation in which all your planning, preparation, and skill resoundingly fell flat?

One of my worst disasters occurred early on in my worship leading career. The music set was well crafted. The band had practiced the arrangements, transition points, and key moments. My comments were carefully groomed to maximize directing the congregation's worship time.

And they responded. Wow! Really responded. Far more exuberantly than in my wildest dreams, or—as it turned out— nightmares.

Apparently the night before someone had left a window cracked open on the upper floor of the building. A small bat entered and found a nice, quiet place to sleep. Apparently the loud music at the peak of our worship set startled him and the little furry fella began swooping and diving throughout the auditorium.

Hands shot up all over the room. People began shouting! Some dove to the floor. Others, young and old, began running the aisles. One man in the balcony began swinging a large trash can in circles above his head, shouting, "I got it, I got it!" But this was no Holy Spirit revival.

There was no recovering from that.[1]

Sometimes, no matter how we try, something we do—even something as insignificant as failing to close a window—impacts the worship experience of others.

The little things

This book focuses a lot on little things. Not that they are unimportant—they're foundationally vital. But they're the kind of things that are easily postponed or ignored. Many worship people may prefer to seek that elusive one big change promising to leapfrog their congregation overnight into the "aha, we've arrived" picture that they visualize when imagining an awesome worship experience.

Most of us have that picture in our mind's eye already.

I've yet to meet anyone serving in worship-arts ministry who can't close their eyes and imagine what their congregation looks like, sounds like, acts like, feels like when everything comes together and everyone is fully engaged, expressing worship to the Lord.

You probably can. What does it look like to you?

While your picture may differ somewhat from the next person's, I'm guessing that your picture doesn't include a terrorized congregation and a little bat flittering about the room.

Mine didn't. But regardless, that pesky little creature changed the day. Our imaginations cannot predict every unexpected detail that we may possibly encounter. Besides, long term impact is often either enabled or disabled by the accumulation of small, seemingly insignificant decisions and their unforeseen consequences.

Here's an example that changed the course of my life.

I remember visiting my wife Anita's family not long after she and I began dating. One day she was away teaching school, and I passed some time at the house observing the various memorabilia she

---

[1] Thank you, Jonathan Miller and Kristin Priest, for corroborating the details of this event, and even though you were both fairly young at the time, it's amazing how those details burned themselves into each of your memories!

displayed about in her room. Trophies for softball pitching, golf, basketball. Many photographs, mostly of friends and family. Her Bible and journal. A partially knit project still attached to a ball of yarn (originally intended as a present to a former boyfriend!). John Michael Talbot and John Denver albums. Hair brushes. Her out-of-tune Ibanez 12-string guitar. Bird and wildflower books. An empty peanut M&M's wrapper. Knickknacks from some of the favorite places where she had lived in New York, Phoenix, Virginia, and Michigan.

As I looked about the room that day, those little mementos reflecting her personality and values clarified into a deeper understanding for me of what made her the person she was. That was the day I realized this gal was someone with whom I could spend the rest of my life.

Kurt Vonnegut said it this way, "Enjoy the little things in life, because one day you will look back and realize they were the big things."

Little things are huge.

That's what this book is about: addressing a handful of easily-postponed, foundational concepts that ultimately shape our effectiveness in accomplishing the work Jesus gives us. *If* we take the time to address them, they can help you reach beyond your current capability and become more the person Jesus set you on the road to become. To steal a phrase from my seventh grade science teacher, "You can actuate your potential."

PAUSE & CONSIDER_____

❑   Which story comes to mind when I think
     about how little things can either make or
     break how effectively I serve?

There's a common trait I've found in people who really knock the ball out of the park when it comes to effective ministry. Here it is. They each address every single one of the concepts we'll look at in these pages. While my "worship heroes" may each approach things differently, the key is that they do it. Even in all the rush and urgency of daily ministry, these champions refuse to compromise.

> *I think that's why so many people who serve never reach their stride. They seem stuck. They have allowed at least one or more of the concepts we'll talk about to remain unaddressed.*

It would be a huge mistake for me to attempt teaching one single, particular formula for successful ministry. That would be a fail right out of the box. Your best approach has to do with you and the Lord, His design, and everything that makes you the person you are now and who you have the potential to become. This book offers observations for your consideration. Besides, I'm still learning. I'm like an assistant on an archeological dig, very curious to see what discoveries you uncover.

I look forward to initiating this transformational conversation. You'll reach your own conclusions. You'll grow. If you're going through this material with a ministry team or one of my thinking partner groups, you'll see the connections between team members increase as you value one another more and come to understand each other's hearts in deeper ways.

It is a joy to realize that you'll be able to accomplish things in ministry outside of my own parameters. That's so exciting! The starting place is just that: the start. The journey extends from there.

PAUSE & CONSIDER_____

❑ What one thing could hinder me from being the best worshiper I'd love to see myself being—if I'd let it?

1.1 THE SLIPPERY MARCH TOWARD BETTER

It's not that people serving in ministry consider things like personal development, perseverance, and teachability unimportant. We say they matter. We believe they matter. But the reality is that many teams take no time to grow in these areas on a regular basis.

We may declare that character, excellence, and so on are of utmost importance, and our ministry manuals (if we have one) may contain pages devoted to their descriptions, values, concepts, and supporting guidelines. However, actually stopping during rehearsal to address them tends to get pushed aside by the urgent grind of creating worship sets week after week. There's just so much to do. Growth slips through the cracks.

I'm guilty!

It reminds me of my struggle with flossing my teeth. It's one of those little things that seems so easy to skip in the urgency of what I want to do next. I've already brushed my teeth, scrubbed my tongue, my breath smells clean, and I'm in a hurry. It's so easy to get out of my flossing habit because the "I'll do it next time" lie to myself gets me out of the bathroom and on with my agenda. But my dentist can always tell, even if I've been good for a month or so leading up to my teeth cleaning appointment. That's because consequences accumulate. The signs eventually show.

We both know it's true.

I want you to enjoy this book much more than a teeth cleaning! Besides, whatever your role in worship-arts ministry, from volunteering as a tech to pastoring a multi-site program, I think you'll agree that you want the personal cost of serving to bring results. And however you measure return-on-investment, I'd willingly bet that you don't want either your gifts or the resulting fruit to be discarded.

If you've served very long at all, you probably have experienced a failed investment or a wasted return. Something came up and you couldn't adequately prepare, so you didn't do as well as you knew you were capable of doing. Or perhaps an announcement ran long and the team had to cut the song for which you had especially worked on, and it felt that your hard work was for nothing. Whether in your control or not, those things happen. It's all part of serving in worship-arts ministry.

Think back to that picture you see when you imagine your congregation fully expressing their hearts in worship. Notice their connectedness. See what they do? They're being impacted by exalting Jesus. Notice how you see yourself. You're probably not frowning, staring blankly ahead, or desperately trying to remember the next chord. You're at the peak of your game. You're effective. Invigorated. Alive. Such a good place to be.

That picture provides a good reason for you to keep on reading. We're moving in that direction.

PAUSE & CONSIDER_____

❑ What about my picture motivates me the
   most?

_____

Carrying on

There may be a gap between the person you see in your picture and the person you see in the mirror. It's O.K. There usually is. It's part of the growth process that comes with serving. God promises that you will grow as you serve. That means you'll change and become more like that picture in your mind. We'll talk about that process in this book, too.

Not everyone reading this is ablaze with passion for worship-arts ministry. Some help in order to meet a need or serve out of a sense of obligation. Others may have volunteered for what seems a long time with little result, and may question whether the return-on-investment was worthwhile. Some of you have seriously contemplated simply walking away from it all.

In two of the churches where I've served overseeing worship-art programs, I discovered that things were way out of whack. People were discouraged, some wounded, some scarred. A few had dropped away. I had to approach those situations like a crisis management counselor. And since that time, I've walked with many people facing tough situations in their own churches. I'm guessing that about everyone who serves eventually gains some scars. Jesus did.

You may have, too.

Intense conflict arises so easily between people serving in worship programs. Let's face it, not only do we work with people who are in process, we're in process, too. What *does* continually surprise me is the tenacity that many people demonstrate by refusing to abandon their hope that things will improve.

We all want our sacrifices to be worthwhile.

I'm encouraged by what the Bible says in Romans 12:1-2.

"Therefore, I urge you, brothers and sisters, in view of God's mercy, to offer your bodies as a living sacrifice, holy and pleasing to God — this is your true and proper worship. Do not conform to the pattern of this world, but be transformed by the renewing of your mind. Then you will be able to test and approve what God's will is — His good, pleasing and perfect will."

I consider this passage to be the official marching orders for worship-arts ministry. We lay down our core—the living vessel containing our being, passions, skills, hopes, ambitions, relationships, history, everything that encompasses what makes up our identity. We do this day after day as a living, breathing expression of worship. It's our gift to God, freely given to Him to do with as He pleases. We do this in a way that meets His approval and fits His purposes. We do it out of love and thanksgiving for His mercy toward us.

And He incorporates into this process our own transformation, removing from within us things that are fleshy, selfish, and have no place in Him. Then He replaces the gaps those things left behind by increasing in us the fruit of His Spirit: love, joy peace, patience, kindness, goodness, gentleness, faithfulness, and self-control. As this process unfolds, we become better aligned with His will, and we understand Him more. It's good, pleasing, and perfect. A great arrangement.

If you think about it, being a living sacrifice is not only the doorway through which we connect our soul to Jesus. It's also how we authentically reach the world.

I realize that although I have not fully "arrived" in all this myself, continuing to work on my next step each day is an attainable process. While the end goal may seem far off and beyond reach, I can take my step for today. Make my good choice. I can do that.

PAUSE & CONSIDER_____

❏ When I think about being the kind of "living sacrifice" I'd like to be, how can a personal challenge that I face possibly impact those around me?

You can make a good choice today, too. Much of the success we will experience both in growing and in serving depends upon the little things we'll talk about in these following pages.

My goal with this book is to share with you an opportunity to think about ways you can make the most of how you invest yourself by serving in ministry. I'm excited to imagine some of the ways you can grow.

Why?

To build you. To build the Church. To impact the world. Mostly to glorify our Lord. That's my deepest motivation.

Think about the brief speck of time each person has on earth to gather the resources from which we'll build our eternal worship of the King. You and I, right now, are building the crown that we will eternally lay at Jesus' feet. It's made from the living fruit that Jesus harvests through us.

I want to give Him the absolutely finest gift possible.

And while we can't take credit for the fruit that Jesus creates, it's an honor to be a first-hand witness and work beside Him. We're the caretakers of His most valuable gems. Someday we get to begin turning them back over to him.

So let's get busy crownsmithing.

Together, we're going to engage in this process as you move forward toward realizing your vision. I want you to shine with nothing to tarnish or hold you back from becoming the champion that Jesus created you to be. Perhaps you will agree that these little things really are the big things after all.

1.2 THE COST OF IMPACT

Everyone makes a difference. Perhaps the statistics are accurate that even a hermit has over 10,000 opportunities to impact others in a lifetime. Certainly you can pass that number. Whether it's your ministry partners, congregants, grocery store clerks, family members, or the waitress at your table, the Lord has built into your day multiple doors through which you are His hands, His feet, His provision of love. Every day—in every encounter—you touch others. How you impact them affects how they impact others. The ripples can be exponential.

You influence.

John Maxwell, named by both Forbes and Inc. Magazines as the world's leading expert on leadership, explained it this way. "After more than five decades of observing leaders around the world and many years of developing my own leadership potential, I have come to this conclusion: *Leadership is influence.* That's it—nothing more, nothing less."

> *One of the great things about making a difference is that you don't have to be aware that you're doing it.*

My high school Sociology class had a field trip to the facility where my severely mentally handicapped cousin was cared for. We walked through his wing while he was being fed. It wasn't a pretty sight. Suddenly something triggered him and he just beamed and laughed in the middle of a spoonful. We never learned his reason, but even through the pudding smeared over his face, you couldn't avoid seeing his unexplained and uncontainable joy. He simply radiated. It was contagious. By the time my class reached the room doors, we were all smiling and walking a bit more lightly.

This happened nearly 4 decades ago, and I still tell the story.

My cousin never recognized me or spoke to me in his entire life. Yet he placed an image that my mind instantly recalls every time I think of the way emotions spread from one person to those around.

That's impact.

I can't help but think that it's safe to assume that you have even more opportunity to impact those around you if you're willing.

You *are* an influencer.

Pulling back from the plow

Whether you lead a team, direct a program, fill a support position, deal with tech, handle logistics, work cameras, or volunteer to move equipment around, your role gives you the opportunity to touch the hearts and minds of others.

When you step on the platform, enter the tech booth, walk backstage, or put on a name tag, people identify you as "someone who knows." They follow your lead.

 Like it or not, that means you are a leader.

Some people serving in worship-arts ministry hungrily embrace the leadership opportunities in ministry; however, many of us hesitate. We're in good company. The Bible is full of such examples. Consider Moses, Gideon, Ester, Timothy, Jonah, Thomas. If you look, I'm sure you can find more.

Many of us are concerned about the consequences of stepping forward once we start considering the cost. It's natural to draw back.

Have you ever found yourself thinking any of these "move-forward killers?"

- I fear that I personally simply am not *enough:* skill and experience, opinions by others, my age, appearance, self-worth, motivation, experience...

- My personal resources are inadequate: time, equipment, money, energy, understanding, relational skills...

- I fear the opportunity doesn't align exactly with my preferences: prefer different roles or responsibilities, like things done differently, issue with leader or teammate...

- I don't want to overstep my boundaries: no one in authority has extended permission by inviting me to influence others or explained the expectations...

You may be able to creatively add a few more excuses to the list.

Sometimes we simply languish indefinitely on the sidelines declaring that we need more prayer or a clearer directive from God, when those bases are already covered. It is easy to fear that tipping point when preparation gives way to embracing the actual risk of stepping forward.

Here's the truth. You actually may not *be* adequate to the task you see coming down the road. You may not feel equipped. You may not feel ready. You may not feel *enough*.

You're probably right.

But here's the good part. You don't need to be adequate. Not the person that you are right now.

It's so easy to forget that God walks beside you. He *is* good enough, and He is the King of New.

That's kind of the point, really. Walking in leadership requires transformation. You will not be the same person in two years that you are now. Development is built into the process, guaranteed. And facing change—becoming someone different than we are now—may be one of the most intimidating things of all, especially if we fear that the Lord may turn us into someone we may not want to become. We don't know the outcome and we're not in control. We may fear that being shaped like clay in a potter's hand is like rolling the dice.

But it's not really the roll of the dice, is it?

If you've walked with the Lord, you can look back at previous growth experiences and see a pattern. You know how He turns situations and experiences with people you've encountered along the way into opportunities for your growth. It's probably cost you something personally, but if you've embraced those opportunities, you've grown. You became more. There's fruit[2] in your life. You've become more like Jesus.

Instead of looking at leadership as costing something that makes you less, it's really the opportunity to exchange some of the yuck within you for something greater than gold. You just have to be willing to let go of that yuck to embrace the next step. Consider the action of letting go to be part of your price of admission.

PAUSE & CONSIDER_____

❑ What could it be like if I could get past the thought or feeling I have that limits my willingness to serve at the level of which I know deep down that I am capable?

---

[2] Spiritual Fruit: love, joy, peace, patience, kindness, gentleness, goodness, faithfulness, and self-control (Galatians 5:22-23)

1.3 LOVING OBEDIENCE—THE SECRET SAUCE

Of course, there's more to successful sustained ministry than sitting back and allowing the Lord to do His work. Most people who serve discover pretty early on that ministry comes at a price. The Bible says in Luke 14:27-29 that disciples should first count the cost of following Jesus. He wants us to continue and finish well. Accepting His call does place some responsibility squarely on our shoulders.

Accountability to the Lord increases. And without being driven by guilt, it is legitimate to acknowledge that He has entrusted to each of us particular resources of gifts, time, energy, and so on. As we give Him a return on that investment, He delights in rewarding us with increased resources and territory to conquer.

Jesus *promises* to make you fruitful *if* you abide in His love for God and for people. That's reason for celebration! Still, He entrusts the obedient "abiding" part to you. Because your influence increases with people when you impact them, should you choose to walk poorly, your actions could devastate them.

The Lord won't just let that slide.

Admittedly, "abiding in God's love" may be a stretch for many of us. It is for me. (Just watch my face when someone cuts me off in traffic!) Even my most compassionate friends confess their need for more. But God is really good at helping us grow, even in the kind of love that enables us to represent Him well to those around us.

Here's one of my favorite examples.

While writing for an internationally-known evangelist, I learned his story of surviving a deadly case of polio as a youth. Despite his debilitating fever, he remembered overhearing the doctor tell his parents to prepare for their son's funeral as he wasn't expected to survive the night. Before slipping into unconsciousness in the darkness of his upstairs room, he vowed that if God spared his life, he would preach the gospel every day.

His parents were amazed the next morning when he miraculously walked down to the landing at the foot of the stairs and asked for something to eat. But it didn't surprise the young man. He knew that God had held up His part of the bargain. After the meal, he went out to the porch, waiting. And sure enough, along came the mailman. So the preaching commenced.

The fire and brimstone message was neither delivered well nor received willingly. When the mailman flatly refused the invitation, the fledgling evangelist said, "Honestly, I don't give a damn. You can go to Hell."

He continued to preach daily, keeping up what he considered to be his half of the deal. He would find someone—anyone—and verbally bludgeon them over the head until they either relented or fled. Mission accomplished.

The results were not positive.

But over the years, as the Lord softened the young man's heart, his impact increased. By the time I first met him he had already led hundreds of thousands of people around the world to the Lord. But first he had to learn to obey in love.

Part of "abiding in Jesus' love" means that sometimes we have the incredible opportunity to partner with Him when He knocks on the door of a person's heart. In whatever role given us, we become a part of Jesus' invitation. How we knock can make a huge difference! We choose what's appropriate, whether mild-mannered tapping, firm rapping, or shaking the door off its hinges.

Although we're not responsible for how others respond to Jesus' invitation offered through us, we ARE responsible that our obedient willingness to knock is accomplished through Jesus' kind of love. The fruit is His job.

Because what we do has far greater impact than the specific words we use, it makes sense that we should consider *how* we interact with others. Our actions matter, even when we don't think others see. Consider your willingness to walk well and remove from yourself any "secret" idols, attitudes, or pet sins. Such things impart to you a vulnerability that the enemy will exploit in an attempt to destroy what God wants to do through you. They clog our spiritual "ears" and desensitize us to recognizing the Lord's lead. Following Jesus means following Him, not following our whim.

PAUSE & CONSIDER

❑ How does the way I approach my role impact other people?

Incrementally growing in abiding in Jesus' love consequently grows our impact upon those we encounter.

1.4 HELP FOR THE LOVING-IMPAIRED

But what about those who—like me—find that loving others can be challenging? I want Jesus' love to touch others through me, but my focus so easily narrows like blinders to my task at hand. In my urgency to address the tasks involved in serving, I sometimes skip connecting relationally. If you've ever overlooked such opportunities because you were too good at getting your job done, you understand.

Yet we loving-impaired servants are not doomed to remain so. The Bible spells out a process in 2 Peter 1: 5-8:

"For this very reason, make every effort to add to your faith goodness; and to goodness, knowledge; and to knowledge, self-control; and to self-control, perseverance; and to perseverance, godliness; and to godliness, mutual affection; and to mutual affection, love. For if you possess these qualities in increasing measure, they will keep you from being ineffective and unproductive in your knowledge of our Lord Jesus Christ."

God knows that many of us sometimes need assistance when it comes to love. He offers a simple growth process. He starts by taking the childlike faith with which we first say "Yes" to Jesus, and begins teaching us to walk in goodness.

He continues, adding to our growth in goodness by helping us work on knowledge, then on self-control, then perseverance, then godliness, then mutual affection. Progress incrementally improves our love capability.

Rather than our being overwhelmed by the challenge of loving like God does, He builds us up step by step. If we follow His process, we will be successful.

> *Jesus assures us that by cooperating with the Holy Spirit's assistance, guidance, and nudging, we will get there. Guaranteed.*

It's not like checking off the box of a to-do list and moving on, never to look back. Wouldn't that be nice! "O.K. our work on knowledge is all done now, everything is now known. Knowledge completed. Now for self-control." No. We continue learning about goodness, perseverance, and godliness. Each quality compounds over time, even while the next one is added and developed. It's a life-long process of continual, incremental movement.

Honestly, thinking about it kind of makes me tired. So much to learn! But I want to stick at it. I *need* these traits to grow in me.

Here's why. This is God's roadmap to becoming effective, and bearing productive fruit is how I honor the Lord.

There's no other way.

As I grow in these areas, I find that even my awareness changes. You may discover the same thing in yourself.

- Our eyes are opened to take advantage of opportunities to influence. We experience a sense of significance when we learn we make a difference.

- Our scope narrows so that we don't become paralyzed or made ineffective by taking on too many priorities.

- We realize our need for help, both from God and from others through whom He provides direction, resources,

19

and encouragement.

- We become more sensitive to the need to align ourselves—our life, behavior, and thinking patterns—with the leader we're becoming rather than with the more limited leader we are now. In other words, we remain open to further transformation.

It's Jesus' call to put down our nets and follow Him. The result? We become His disciples and join Him in His work. His goals become ours. The unfolding process of our being transformed glorifies Jesus, and lives are changed on an eternal scope.

PAUSE & CONSIDER_____

❑ When I consider an area of serving-related inadequacy in my life, what difference could result from God's transformation?

_____

Saying "Yes" to Jesus, enters you front and center into the transformational arena of influencing those around you. You become His ambassador, His hands, His pipeline of love.

1.5 CONSIDER YOUR GOAL (HINT: IT'S TRANSFORMATION!)

The real question isn't whether or not you are a person of influence, a leader. The actual question is "How will you lead?" Despite the countless times we've all witnessed the damaging results from poor leadership, that continues to be the model followed by so many leaders—even in ministry.

Early in his reign, young King Solomon faced this same dilemma. Although his father had accumulated significant wealth through a lifetime of successful military conquest, Solomon knew firsthand the turmoil played out amongst his siblings and the consequences upon the entire country. Reigning for about three years after King David's death gave Solomon a taste for the challenges he would continue to face for the remainder of his reign as he dealt with religious issues, internal and international politics, and family intrigue.

At this point God offered a special blessing that Solomon himself could select. The Bible records his response in 1 Kings 3:7-10:

"'Now, Lord my God, you have made your servant king in place of my father David. But I am only a little child and do not know how to carry out my duties. Your servant is here among the people you have chosen, a great people, too numerous to count or number. So give your servant a discerning heart to govern your people and to

distinguish between right and wrong. For who is able to govern this great people of yours?' The Lord was pleased that Solomon had asked for this."

King Solomon understood that the fruit of his choices would directly impact everyone within his sphere of influence. Although you and I may not rule a kingdom, we each have opportunity to leave a significant thumbprint on the lives around us.

We each face King Solomon's daunting question. "What will be the consequence of my life upon others?"

J.R. Miller captured the significance of this thought with clarity.

"There have been meetings of only a moment which have left impressions for life, for eternity. No one of us can understand that mysterious thing we call influence... yet out of every one of us continually virtue goes, either to heal, to bless, to leave marks of beauty; or to wound, to hurt, to poison, to stain other lives."[3]

We probably agree that ultimately God creates the fruit. Even so, we still play an important part. As for me, I want to embrace His lead and participate. And although I'm not sure that it's supposed to work this way, part of my sense of significance comes from the knowledge that by choosing to follow my Creator, I am working in the Father's family business.

Perhaps you feel similarly. You can choose to follow His lead, too, take up your hammer (or guitar), and be about His Kingdom Construction Company work.

The Lord desires to share with you what matters most to His heart. But He invites rather than demands. That's one reason why He made you to be the gatekeeper of your soul. You are the one in charge of permitting Him to open doors into the various rooms of your heart and allowing Him to create change there by expanding your thinking, igniting your passion, implanting vision. He knocks and waits. You alone permit or deny access. Only you. His knocking may even grow urgent, but he will not violate this condition.

---

[3] J.R. Miller, *The Every Day of Life* (New York: Thomas Y. Crowell, 1892), 246-47.

To grow or not to grow - that is *your* question

By entrusting us to steward our own growth, God grants us *choice*. He instigates growth opportunities. We either move with it or reject it. Wow—it's an awe-filling thing to be handed power like that with such far-reaching consequences!

Even so, perhaps you have allowed an opportunity to slip through your fingers. I know I have.

Thankfully, the Lord remains faithful. Instead of giving up, God is patient. He loves us enough to offer an additional opportunity, then another, then another, until at the end of the day we realize we've been walking and never reaching the one place He wants us to go. He even redeems what we may consider to be extreme circumstances to help us realize our need to move forward to become more fully the creatures of joy, peace, and love that He envisioned while He first breathed into us His gift of life.

While it may grieve His heart, our struggles never surprise God. The Apostle Paul focused on this battle in Romans 7:15. He says:

"I do not understand what I do. For what I want to do I do not do, but what I hate I do."

It seems that he gets really personal in this chapter. He confesses in Romans 7:21-25:

"So I find this law at work: Although I want to do good, evil is right there with me. For in my inner being I delight in God's law; but I see another law at work in me, waging war against the law of my mind and making me a prisoner of the law of sin at work within me. What a wretched man I am! Who will rescue me from this body that is subject to death? Thanks be to God, who delivers me through Jesus Christ our Lord!"

Paul recognized that his transformational struggle exceeded his ability to resolve. I find this comforting because at least I'm in good company. Paul's solution? Embrace Jesus, the One who conquered bondage, death, and sin.

Keith Green's old song "So you wanna go back to Egypt?"

23

captured the tenacity with which many of us fight growth. Perhaps at times it appears easier to retrace the path returning to old chains than to put in the work required to take the promised land.

God never wastes our pain.
Unfortunately, sometimes we do.

Instead of continuing the cycle, wouldn't it be better to grasp everything God has for us this round? We don't have to make the trip again. Seize this day—today—and take full advantage of the adversity you face to embrace what God has in mind to teach.

God often allows us to set the pace of our growth and to ultimately choose to follow Him. He's taken all eternity to prepare the next 30 seconds of our existence. Yes, there are circumstances beyond our control, as well as consequences for the actions of ourselves and others, but sooner or later, in every event, we have to face the question, "Am I going to pay the price to follow where God is leading so that I can embrace what He has ahead?"

It can be easy to declare ahead of time how committed followers we are, but—at least for me—sometimes when the time actually comes to put feet to faith and follow the cloud, it can be intimidating to accept the great adventure and step into an unknown sea where—if God doesn't show up and be God—I'm doomed to drown.

He gives us the opportunity to make the good choice for whatever decision we face. He doesn't make the choice for us. He doesn't trick us to walk His path. Although He knew our decisions before we were ever born, we are the ones who get to make those choices.

You're making them now.

He tirelessly knocks on the door of your heart by using the doorbells of relationships, occupations, finances, anything of significance in your world. Even that person cutting you off in traffic. The Lord wants to partner with you and together develop your character. This vital, ongoing, transformational process aligns you with Him and with the fruit He promises to create through you in the lives of others. For those of us serving in worship-arts, our transformation process often occurs right in the middle of ministry.

He knew that from the instant we failed in the garden that growth would remain hard for us. But I don't think He looks at this process as a difficulty for which we should grit our teeth, gather our strength, and trudge grimly ahead. You see, He remains steadfastly determined to share with us His celebration banquet, even in the valley of the shadow of death before the very face of an enemy determined to defile and destroy anything God values. And how He loves us! He treasures our hearts and grieves for our pain more than we even experience, and He delights in walking with us through challenges. The creator of the entire universe treasures every moment you spend together, including the tough times.

You will impact people. And you will be transformed in turn. This perpetual transformation process matters deeply to God. You may or may not agree, but I believe that this—at its very core—is the primary thing that ministry is all about. The more you become like Jesus, the better you reflect Him, and the more you honor Him.

PAUSE & CONSIDER_____

❑   When was a time that I experienced a significant sense of freedom after releasing myself to the Lord? How did that moment feel? What did the Lord add into my life? What tries to hinder me from experiencing that right now?

1.6 THE LONG, UNWINDING ROAD

Have you ever felt like you should have learned a lesson from the Lord much, much sooner than you actually did?

Perhaps you've experienced something similar to what I felt when I struggled for two weeks trying to remember that I needed to slow my car's speed to 25 miles per hour on Boyne City's Lake Street. I kept forgetting. But I learned quite quickly when those red and blue flashing lights appeared in my rear view mirror.

But other times it seems that it takes time to learn something significant from the Lord because He needs to prepare our minds to receive what He wants to show us. Occasionally part of our learning process requires that we work through several layers of lesser understandings before the actual, deeper truth crystallizes into focus.

> *Some of the lessons we value most came at the greatest price.*

When Jesus was trying to impart to His disciples the foundational truth that He was indeed the Messiah, He didn't simply say, "I am the Messiah." He knew that they needed to come to this conviction for themselves. They had to own it personally. The rest of their lives would build upon that realization.

There's something we can learn by taking a look at how Jesus helped them through the learning curve.

Jesus used a gentle, unfolding process to reveal this truth with the disciples. He started by sending out the disciples to get their hands dirty and apply for themselves what they had already learned from their initial time with him. They came back to excitedly report that it worked! He then performed a series of miracles though which the disciples understood that he was Lord of the Sabbath, of provision, of the elements, and of our bodies.

Eventually he warmed up to the big question of his identity by starting with the safer question of what the disciples had heard others say about Jesus' identity. Then he made it personal. "Who do *you* say that I am?" Peter nailed it, "You are the Messiah, the Son of the Living God." Jesus confirmed Peter's comprehension, stating that upon this rock—this truth—Jesus would build the Church.

That had to have been such a shining moment for Peter!

> *Studying Jesus' learning process for the disciples keeps leading me to this key foundational concept: I am increasingly convinced that ministry—at its very core— is all about transformation.*

That thought is really the heart of this book. (If you're a person who highlights or underlines while you read, I'm strongly hinting that you use a little ink right about now!) This certainly has been the most challenging chapter to write (and possibly to read)! But this concept really matters for your own growth and for the growth of those you serve. So I'll write it again.

Ministry is about transformation.

This concept did not sink in for me overnight. It took a while to comprehend. It took years! Perhaps my slow learning curve had something to do with being continually distracted by important-but-lesser goals. I can be so easily distracted by getting the tasks done.

Looking back, I discover that I had slipped into leading my churches and team as if I had forgotten what ultimately mattered to the Lord regarding my worship role. It's not that what I spent my time focusing on was out of line. But my primary focus had shifted by spending my primary energy on things that ultimately were secondary. If you would have looked at the way I functioned, you would have recognized these as my top priorities.

As you read this list, consider what your behaviors and time allocation say about your real focus.

5 misguided motives that miss the mark

1. Worship is about **me** (my crafted expression or interaction with God, my sense of satisfaction, performance, sacrifice, learning, obedience, preparation, accomplishment of the job).

2. Worship is about **the team** connecting with one another to create something greater than any of us could bring individually.

3. Worship is about **the staff**'s role in preparing the congregation, in bringing unity, in inviting them to engage, and in reinforcing core beliefs and values.

4. Worship is about **the congregation** (their worship experience, their relational connection, their group expression of interacting with God, their level of engagement, and attracting others).

5. Worship is about **the expression itself** as we declare truths about Him and craft an appropriate praise offering to glorify Him for what He does (the song, the production, the roadmap, the flow, the art).

Over the years I've also heard other things listed as worship's goal. You may think of other motives to add.

Each of these considerations have legitimate merit. They're actually pretty important. But they fight for our attention, time, energy. And sometimes, even when we try to have our own safeguards in place, they can take the wheel.

They cannot fulfill the *Big Why*—the reason that the Lord made us to be His working partners in the garden.

Our going about His business is simply the opportunity to walk with Him. Doing that with our attention focused squarely on Him unfettered by these distractions, means something really important happens. We become more the one He created us to be.

PAUSE & CONSIDER_____

❑ Which important-but-lesser goals do I have which I must carefully handle to keep from becoming distracted from what's ultimately important?

1.7 WHY HE'S A'KNOCKIN'

It stands to reason that spending time with the Creator of the Universe will be transformative. How can it not be? His character rubs off. Our character becomes more conformed to the likeness of Jesus. Besides, if you're connecting people with the fire that is the Holy Spirit, shouldn't you be impacted as well?

There is a simple reason why He paid so dearly for our transformation.

He loves us.

That concept remains first and foremost in God's mind. It infiltrates every interaction between us. I sometimes feel sad for the burden it places upon Him. I can be so thick headed that I must frustrate Him at times. Thankfully His grace is greater than my comprehension. He overcomes my limitations by providing additional opportunities to grow.

George McDonald considered God's love to be His primary motive for our creation and development. While the wording of this quote is a bit tricky—what written in the 1800's isn't?—something significant hides in these lines.

"Love loves unto purity. Love has ever in view the absolute loveliness of that which it beholds. Where loveliness is incomplete, and love cannot love its fill of loving, it spends itself to make more lovely, that it may love more; it strives for perfection, even that itself may be

perfected—not in itself, but in the object.... Therefore all that is not beautiful in the beloved, all that comes between and is not in love's kind, must be destroyed. And our God is a consuming fire."[4]

In other words, Jesus loves his bride and helps whatever is lovely in her to blossom. He is worthy of her perfection and He is determined to see her complete, whole, and beautiful. Anything marring or coming between the groom and His bride is His mortal enemy. For her, He paid the ultimate price, and He will not be denied. I love—and am terrified by—McDonald's biblical reference to Deuteronomy 4:24 and Hebrews 12:28-29, warning in the last line. "And our God is a consuming fire."

Jesus takes our transformation seriously. It makes sense that we should, too. You know what He sacrificed to make it possible.

The Bible reminds us of this in Ephesians 5:25-27:

"Christ loved the church and gave himself up for her to make her holy, cleansing her by the washing with water through the word, and to present her to himself as a radiant church, without stain or wrinkle or any other blemish, but holy and blameless."

Jesus is fully committed to this transformation. He did not expect the Church to transform on her own. So one great help He provided to us comes in the form of gifting us with leader-guides.

The Bible says in Ephesians 4:11-13:

"So Christ himself gave the apostles, the prophets, the evangelists, the pastors and teachers, to equip his people for works of service, so that the body of Christ may be built up until we all reach unity in the faith and in the knowledge of the Son of God and become mature, attaining to the whole measure of the fullness of Christ."

Regardless of how you doctrinally define *apostles*, *prophets*, *evangelists*, *pastors*, and *teachers*, this passage clearly designates these roles as one of the Lord's primary provisions to the church for a laser-

---

[4] George MacDonald, Unspoken Sermons, First Series: The Consuming Fire.

specific task. They equip people for works of service. If we're going to serve, these folks are there so we can do it better.

What's the big deal? God's reason for such a gift?

Jesus knew that on our own we simply are not enough. We must become more than we currently are in order to meet the task. More of Him needs to shine through us, and too much of our selves gets in the way.

But that's O.K. He's not worried. He developed a way for us to become more. And to top it off, He gives us helpers in the form of these individuals charged with His directive to coach, nurture, instruct, and even prod us along. With their assistance, we can be built up until we all radiate Jesus. We transform.

Ministry itself positions us squarely amidst becoming Christ-like. Embracing transformation—both for yourself and for those you serve—is one of the characteristics that differentiate ministry from hobby. It can be overwhelming if we stop for a moment to appreciate how incredibly awesome it is that the God of all creation chooses to invite us as junior partners as He impacts the world. He sends us as His hands to represent His touch to those around us! You are a gift whom the Lord Himself has provided to serve the Church.

Consider that for a moment. It really matters.

In my mind I can imagine the Lord saying to the angels, "Hey, look, they're going to need some help to walk with me, and I'm doing something special. I've got just the right person in mind. No one else is a better fit. See who I picked!"

He selected you.

Whether or not you serve in a position of oversight, this message is vital for you. Your spiritual growth depends upon it.

According to this passage, how does the body of Christ become built up? It's right there in black and white.

Your growth is not provided by apostles, prophets, evangelists, pastors, and teachers. They're just around to help equip you for the task. Your growth occurs when you serve. That's how you mature.

Your leaders equip you for service. You serve. You grow. You become more like Jesus. Rinse and repeat.

Such a simple challenge! But we both know how daunting it can be. That's why we can say along with the Apostle Paul, "Thanks be to God, who delivers me through Jesus Christ our Lord!"

Jesus is firmly, completely, ultimately committed to our growth. He gave us His Word. He gave us His blood. He provided us with the Holy Spirit as our guide along the way. Although it seems to require about everything we can muster, with His help the gold at the end is worth the effort.

PAUSE & CONSIDER_____

❑ What price did I pay for my own most recent point of transformation?

1.8 TAKING TIME

I continually find myself wishing for a fast track to growth. I'd like to find the express route and bypass all the effort and time. I'm probably not alone.

Growth doesn't work that way. It usually comes gradually. I sometimes have to remind myself that the journey itself provides precious moments of intimacy with the Lord. "Yes, He my King, the holy, powerful, awesome, and fearful God Almighty." But the journey serves to remind me that He is also my ever-present guide, my sergeant in arms, my encourager, my constant companion.

Besides, the Lord wants us to survive the process. Instead of overwhelming a person with 10,000,000 changes to become like Jesus, the Holy Spirit usually picks one or two to work on at a time. He surrounds us with situations and people so we recognize the need to embrace growth in that area. Lasting growth takes time, and sometimes we need many opportunities.

I sometimes wish the Lord would make it a bit easier. GPS easy. That's the ticket. He could just lead us around like a spiritual GPS. "Turn right. Continue. Warning, slow traffic ahead; recalculating. Use right lane to exit and turn right. Ding! You are mature."

Wouldn't that make things easier?

But I find that it's more like my GPS experience in Kentucky. For 11 months while taking a break from ministry I traveled the highways and byways designing and installing security systems. I heavily relied on my trusty GPS. That is, until the day when after driving 3 hours to meet my customer, I stopped at the dead end of a rocky dirt road surrounded by pasture. My trusty GPS cheerfully announced, "You have arrived!" No house in sight. Not even a barn. That's when my cell-phone signal died.

Yes, God's answer book guides our path. But it doesn't spell out every choice in clear-cut, black-and-white, no-questions-asked detail. As we meditate on it, the Lord reveals Himself and His ways. Digging deep into it helps align our values with His.

> *The Bible* accompanies *our journey, rather than dictates our steps because the Word is Jesus made flesh. He doesn't want readership; He wants relationship.*

And nothing can separate us from His love.

God doesn't merely give us a spiritual GPS, an easy answer to mindlessly follow. Isn't it better to engage in life, to participate along the way?

Jesus doesn't want an automaton. He wants a Bride. A partner. Someone with whom He walks in the cool of the day. In my imagination, where it's so easy for me to picture myself getting things right, I see him whispering his invitation to me, and I imagine my immediate recognition of his voice and willing response, not out of obedience or obligation, but out of pure love and joy for being aligned with my Lord.

Yes, that's how I imagine it.

Unfortunately it doesn't seem to always go that smoothly. I'm like my own worst enemy. My thick skull gravitates toward appeasing my own selfishness.

Thankfully the Lord doesn't give up when I miss His gentle nudging. He simply raises the stakes to better get my attention, and gives me another opportunity. I admit that I've gotten all the way to the "whacked over the head with a 2x4" stage, and a few times even beyond that to the "Category 5 Hurricane" life disaster. At such times, the cost that I—and consequentially those around me—must pay for transformation increases proportionately.

In the book *Draw the Circle*[5], Mark Batterson puts it this way.

"We tend to view the goal as the goal, but in God's economy, the process is the goal. It's not about what we're doing at all; it's about who we're becoming in the process. It's not about doing great things for God; it's about God doing great things in us."

Ministry is all about transformation. God designed it to help us grow. The role itself is merely a catalyst.

Consider how things would be different if the Lord's love for us was finite or conditional. But it remains unquenchable. He loves us enough to use extremes if necessary to help us embrace transformation. You know the price willingly He paid—our growth is that important.

PAUSE & CONSIDER_____

❑ How can I ensure moments of personal interaction with Jesus that allow me to recognize and embrace transformation?

---

5 Thank you, Audrey Laureys, for introducing Mark's book to me. I'm challenged each time I read it!

1.9 A CULTURE OF BECOMING

It's not hard to test the truth of God's promise that growth follows service. Search through your memories and pull out your mental "Great Moments in Serving" highlight reel. Do those times coincide with an increase in your life of love, joy, peace, patience, kindness, goodness, gentleness, faithfulness, or self-control?

They usually do.

That's part of the fruit of harvest in your life. It's a kind of ministry natural law. Growth follows service. When true, full-life service happens, growth in some shape or form isn't far behind.

However, perhaps the opposite principle is also true: minimal service results in minimal growth.

What about the times in life when there doesn't seem to be much increase in fruit?

Do you ever wonder why some people seem to go years without experiencing much spiritual deepening?

Perhaps they are not serving in a significant or sacrificial way.

Growth is built into serving. It's a natural byproduct, a spiritual consequence put into place by our Creator. Instead of becoming less by giving ourselves away to the Lord, He helps us become more. It's built into the process.

> *It's Jesus' promise. Obedient sacrificial*
> *service cultivates maturing growth.*

I think that's awesome!

It's also a bit daunting, especially if you want to help others grow. Consider this. When you serve, you grow. But when you influence someone else to serve, you open for them the door into a primary vehicle through which the Lord activates growth in His Bride. You become a part of Jesus' transforming touch upon them.

And when we're each growing in this way, and sharing our growth—being a part of one another's growth—the culture that results from our shared development becomes contagiously dynamic. Jesus loves to see this in His Bride as we experience Him together.

This ripples out to touch an exponentially increasing number of people on an eternal scale. We're talking serious impact on a scale of revival!

Opportunity void

The only problem is that a lot of the time things don't really look like that.

Do you ever wonder why there seems to be times when the Church lacks the intensity that comes when people experience radical transformation? Why do our youth sometimes walk away and accuse Christianity of being more about religious behavior than about true change?

Perhaps we should consider that somewhere along the way we've lost our "culture of becoming."

Is it possible that we can slide into being so busy about our own serving responsibilities, that we fail to notice the chance to allow others to play the game? We might let them help us to get our part done, but do we sometimes become spiritual service ball-hogs who cannot pass the ball to our teammates?

I'm thinking that when this happens, true growth for everyone has stalled.

I wrestle with this thought a lot.

This clarified for me one day while talking with a representative from an organization that helps churches strategically hire key leaders, he shook his head and sadly admitted, "Tim, I work with churches all across the country every day, and unfortunately many times—whether small or large—church overseers seem far more interested in the appearance of the person on the platform than in that person's capability to actually move the Church forward."

How tragic!

When he said this, my mind immediately began leaping down the style-over-substance rabbit hole, but suddenly an even bigger issue came into view, at least for me personally, and possibly for you, too.

Ponder for a moment. It makes sense that people lacking substance but having high-value skill sets may seem attractive initially. Such talent makes the rest of us address jealousy. Still, common sense suggests that programs lacking substance often eventually crash.

But what about the competent people? I'm talking about those of us who can get the job done well and keep things running smoothly to everyone's satisfaction. Is there a different kind of lack of substance that we fall into?

I recognize that for someone like me—a person who is pretty confident in overseeing a worship program and getting the job done—it can be so easy to slip into the busy, preoccupying rush of production that tends to insulate someone like me from including others in the specific tasks we do well. At those moments those of us who are "someone like me" fail to help others to engage in growth.

The job gets done, but on a growth level everyone loses!

Worship people often feel intense pressure to get things right. You know what I'm talking about. Nothing can slip. We keep so many plates spinning and one miscalculation may cause the whole thing to crash. You may have run into this for yourself.

I've often heard it said that the buck stops with the staff. That makes sense. We're responsible—and sometimes paid—to provide excellence, complete the check list of tasks for the day, and meet our own personal expectations. But it seems that sometimes our drive to provide excellence may hinder us from entrusting vital serving opportunities to the people we lead.

I'm guilty. Probably even more than I realize. But my failure to engage, trust, and invest in others doesn't change this key truth.

Serving remains the doorway through which maturity often enters.

If that's true, then whether holding an "official" leader's title or simply holding a broom, our real task is to facilitate growth opportunities for our people. That's the job-behind-our-job.

I realize that each of us must find a balance. But as deadlines loom, we often hear the call of expediency inside our heads, demanding, "Just take over and get the job done!"

Submitting to that voice means dropping the door on growth for someone else. The door closes upon their opportunity to become more like Jesus through engaging now. I hate to admit it, but I know I have caught myself wearing such blinders of urgency.

PAUSE & CONSIDER_____

❏   What is lost when I turn down an opportunity to incorporate others when I serve? What impact can I envision if my congregation developed a "culture of becoming?"

1.10 BEYOND THE BLINDERS

My friend Glenn serves at a church where I worship pastored. As I prepared the manuscript for this book, he reminded me of an experience we shared that I think exemplifies the impact of blinders. Glenn said:

"I remember one particular rehearsal session you tracked me down in the parking lot after I had a bit of a silent meltdown and was sitting in my car about to leave. I had wanted your help to take care of a problem with my in-ears, but you were repeatedly pulled away. I had been having one of those Especially Chaotic Days following a really bad week and was just not in a good place mentally. I was hurting. I felt ignored over something that was probably a simple fix. I realize that you were just had a lot of things going on all at once. You didn't know the burden I was carrying that night from the rest of the week because I'm a guy who doesn't discuss those sorts of things. I reacted the way I did because I'm still in process. We—I—have to communicate effectively and forgive because—as you said—we all want to improve. Not only are those we work with still in process, we're in process, too. We're all in process. It's so important to remember that when there is a conflict.[6]"

Glenn was struggling with a simple in-ear issue during some chaotic moments at rehearsal. I allowed myself to keep getting

---

[6] Thank you, Glenn, for your willingness to share this great example!

distracted by things that I judged at the time to be more urgent, and I neither finished helping him with the issue nor asked a sound tech to address it. I was wearing blinders.

Perhaps I assumed that Glenn's issue wasn't that big of a deal. Under normal circumstances, it wouldn't have been. However, because this event occurred in the context of a particularly difficult week at Glenn's stressful workplace where he responds to 911 emergency calls, the intensity level jumped significantly. My blinders kept me focused elsewhere, and I missed the opportunity to connect with Glenn relationally until the situation escalated.

Does this kind of situation sound familiar?

I almost didn't follow Glenn into the parking lot. I rationalized that he likely needed time alone to pull things together. But thankfully the Lord nudged past my blinders—I think a more sensitive band member pointed out that Glenn hadn't stepped out to the bathroom and was actually heading home—and for that brief and shining moment I did the right thing and sought him out. Instead of losing him that day, he continues to grow and increase in impact. I'm very grateful for that.

That choice offered us an opportunity to move forward. Glenn was reminded that I care about him. He learned to share more openly about himself and to check his expectations of others. I learned that once again I needed to offload some tasks so that I could connect better relationally. The whole team learned that unity matters. Isn't that a practical example of growth and unity-building in action? Thanks for sticking with me, Glenn!

Sharing the joy

When someone says "Yes" to Jesus, a deep transformation runs to the core of their being with huge ramifications. This new believer instantaneously becomes part of the Bride of Christ. Serving intrinsically extends from that new identity, fully capable of producing Jesus-sized fruit.

Like worship itself, serving expresses who we have become. We are not *in* the Church; we *are* the Church. Everywhere we go, whatever we do, whomever we encounter, we are the Bride of Christ. In the grocery store line. Changing traffic lanes. Holding a crying child in the church nursery whose diaper overflowed long before the child was dropped off. We reflect Jesus.

When you answer Jesus' knock to serve, the Holy Spirit gets busy. And when other people join in, we all usually benefit.

Whether you hold an oversight position entrusted with directing others, or simply help set up microphone stands, your role provides you with the opportunity to facilitate others to serve and enable that growth process to unfold.

Fostering a "culture of becoming" may be as simple as asking, "Here Joe, could you help me move these mic stands to the closet?"

Even so, I find that it remains so hard, especially for me at least, to avoid the temptation to just take care of things myself. I know how I like things to be done, and I have the skills and experience to work efficiently. I don't want to bother other people. Plus I want to know that the job actually was completed instead of falling through the cracks when a well-intentioned volunteer became distracted and forgot. So I literally have to remind myself that whenever I do move into "get 'er done" autopilot mode, I may rob people of the Lord's opportunity for them to be who they are—the Church—and possibly experience growth in some way that I may not even see.

The Bible encourages us in Ephesians 4:14-16 by saying:

"Then we will no longer be infants, tossed back and forth by the waves, and blown here and there by every wind of teaching and by the cunning and craftiness of people in their deceitful scheming. Instead, speaking the truth in love, we will grow to become in every respect the mature body of him who is the head, that is, Christ. From him the whole body, joined and held together by every supporting ligament, grows and builds itself up in love, as each part does its work."

According to this passage, spiritual growth results when you do your work as part of the Church body. But transforming your maturity level doesn't happen on its own. You have to say "yes" and engage by investing yourself into that work—call it "significant sacrificial service."

When you serve in this way, especially working together alongside others, one way the Lord accelerates your growth is to use that interaction with others to bring areas within yourself to your attention—"fleshy" bits that need His redemptive touch. For me, that means addressing my selfishness, pride, or impatience. We each have our own issues.

As He works with us in the serving environment, and we respond to His invitation to address our growth areas, He increases the fruit of His Spirit in our lives.

I love that while I grow in a particular area, those I serve with are also growing. We grow simultaneously, albeit possibly in different areas. So not only is there fruit that comes directly from what the Lord accomplishes through my serving, but there is also the result of what the Lord accomplishes through others. Our growth and what we accomplish together join in a "sum is greater than the parts" kind of multiplication.

So significant sacrificial service, especially when partnering with others, results in a huge harvest on many levels. That's a great win!

What can I do about blinders that possibly affect my willingness to embrace my current point of transformation? How may my growth be increased through my building others?

PAUSE & CONSIDER_____

❑ What can I do about blinders that possibly
   affect my willingness to embrace my
   current point of transformation? How may
   my growth be increased by my building
   others?

44

2

THE TOOLBOX WITHIN

2.0 PEOPLE OF CHARACTER

No conversation about being the best you can be in worship ministry could be complete without a person taking a look under the hood to examine the tools they have. Are the right tools there? What condition are they in? Is anything missing? None of us want to be ill-equipped.

We each share a matching identity in Christ. We all have the same value as priceless masterpieces in His eyes. But that's about where the similarities end. We look different, sound different, think different, smell different. We're each unique in our own blend of personality, interest, motive, skill, resources, and much more. Yet the Lord calls us together into a cohesive unit that He expects to reach the world.

One of the keys making this miracle possible is the Lord's transforming work in our *character*. After all, that's where God's changes show up in us. And the greatest character trait, according to 1 Corinthians 13 is—and you know this—love.

I remember so clearly standing around in the campfire light as a third grader in 1970 singing "They Will Know We Are Christians By Our Love." At the time, the song was only 4 years old and far too contemporary for most church services, but it grabbed my young heart and—at least for me—declared how the Church could reach the world. By our love.

Contrast that with the fact that in two of my last three worship positions I had to immediately address helping people heal from ministry-related conflict. Working with church teams around the country revealed similar challenges.

I find it heartbreaking to admit that far too often the impact of Christians in ministry upon others may by neutral or negative. If you jump online to any worship-related Facebook page, it won't take long to find someone's post dealing with damage caused by people impacting one another poorly. And this is in worship-arts ministry!

We could blame communication breakdowns, conflicting values, stressors caused by balancing ministry with the rest of life, and so on. These factors do raise legitimate concerns worth addressing. But they are not the cause of negative impact.

Poor impact stems directly from underdeveloped character.

One way or another, you *will* impact people. Isn't it worthwhile to make sure your impact positively points people to the Lord?

Developing your character aligns you with how Jesus wants to touch the world through you.

More than anything else, *character* remains the number one factor determining the sustained impact your life will have. Building your character is the essence of personal discipleship. Programs, values, skills, presentations, planning, knowledge—nothing else will so greatly affect your long term results.

But for some reason we just put it off.

Hey, let's talk about chara... Squirrel!

It's not that we don't value building character. We don't even mind talking about it sometimes. But it doesn't seem to stick.

I'm guilty. One afternoon at a large national worship conference I became inspired and actually skipped what I considered to be more exciting workshops to go attend the workshop on character building.

On purpose. I don't know what got into me.

Everyone in the room paid complete attention to the speaker. We all agreed that character matters. We clapped at the end and took his materials. On the way out, we felt pretty good and congratulated ourselves for doing our duty. But this was my conversation walking out of the room:

"Great session. I've really got to apply that. Oh no! He ran long and now I'm missing the live demo in the exhibition hall on those incredible patches from the new Bethel album...."

I still remember how to modify the keyboard patch EQ settings, but I don't remember the character workshop content. Go figure.

It's not startling news. Character development just doesn't rate high on our long "What I must get done today" list. It's kind of like eating lima beans. I'll do it if I have to. But I'd rather be eating steak.

It seems so much more *urgent* to focus instead upon building impeccable skill, drawing others into deep experiences, crafting what seems like soul-awakening music, relational team building... almost anything but the long, painful, and uncelebrated drudgery of building our own character.

I don't recall anyone ever asking, "Did you develop your character today?" Something in me certainly fights it—or at least tries directing my attention elsewhere. Can you relate?

Developing your character enables your long term impact. It's also your protection.

An apple a day

Why do so many ministry leaders fall flat, run out of steam, lose their team, or burn out in a fireball of scandal? No one seems to be exempt, regardless of how promising their start, how skilled their tool box, how polished their presentation, how preeminent their accomplishments. Sadly, disappointingly, it still happens. Leaders fail. We're all vulnerable. Continually, imminently vulnerable.

Even worship people.

And the danger isn't limited to the person running the program. Support staff and volunteers face the same thing.

I've personally seen spiritual leaders overcome by pride, hunger for money, refusal to change, adultery, self-advancement, addiction, lack of accountability, and lack of self-discipline. Every time, people's lives were shattered, and the damage was not limited to those directly involved. The face of Jesus' Bride was blemished before the whole world.

Everyone pays.

Whenever what's going on inside us becomes inadequate to handle what's going on outside us, the meltdown clock starts ticking. This is key. Our inside character must outshine our activity and who we present ourselves to be. Character enables us to walk with authentic integrity. Character dresses us in the armor necessary to face an enemy aggressively committed to defile anything that glorifies our Lord. Character gives us the push necessary to persist and sustainably attain our goals.

Team building, declaring values, training skills, and program development all amount to nothing unless the people implementing them focus first and foremost on developing their own character.

Inside trumps Outside. Always.

If your character grows, so will your capacity to love. Maybe if enough of us do that, then they really can know that we are Christians by our love.

PAUSE & CONSIDER_____

❑   In what way could I be tempted to
    present myself as bigger on the
    outside than I suspect I really may be
    on the inside?

_____

2.1 THE PRESENT AND FUTURE YOU

Unfortunately, we are not automatically instilled with exemplary character the moment we're born, get a driver's license, graduate, marry, have children, or retire. Neither is it imparted to us when we become a Christian. Like a diamond, Godly character develops over time under extreme pressure.

Besides, the concern of a lifetime of ministry collapsing in the flames of sin seems so remote, especially for those not nurturing a secret sin or harboring dark skeletons in the closet. (Thank the Lord for the times He protected us from ourselves!) However, I remind myself that those who became entangled in such activity probably never set out deliberately to do so.

I can't imagine hearing a child announcing, "When I grow up I want to build an international ministry and then become an addict and see it all fall apart."

Continual character development provides a layer of protection and builds the kind of credibility to which people respond. Mature character legitimizes that you have something valuable to teach because you've wrestled through learning that something for yourself.

Developed character wields greater potency than any well-intentioned slogan printed on a poster of a kitten.

Successful long-term ministry rises and falls with character development. It's your doorway to influence.

PAUSE & CONSIDER_____

❑ What pressures best help me focus
   on my own character development?

_____

Meet the Potential You

Consider David during the time King Saul hunted him in the wilderness. This challenging period of constant life-threatening danger became the forge in which David's character solidified.

Years before, God's prophet had anointed David to become king, but he did not yet wear the crown. David refused to take matters prematurely into his own hands although he had opportunity to assassinate King Saul.

But when Israel's borders were overrun by their enemy and a city was being raided with vital food stores stolen, David didn't act like "David the fugitive running from King Saul." Instead he rescued the town. While King Saul was preoccupied with hunting him down, fugitive David behaved like a king should.

> *David aligned himself with the man he was anointed to become instead of limiting himself to the man he already was.*

Therein lies a huge key to character development. Wow—I need that concept in my life!

Can you imagine a picture in your mind of the person God created you to be? I'm not talking about some fantasy character from a daydream; I'm talking about the unfettered person you know deep down that the Lord designed you to become. Your skills are trained and operating at peak performance. You're focused, comfortable, and undistracted. You sense God's nudging and follow with confidence. Other people are reached and impacted through you in vital ways, and because of your influence they in turn impact other people.

Isn't that a good picture? Think about it for a moment. Consider the nuances. How you stand. How you make eye contact. How you sound. The picture you are imagining is a picture of the potential you.

Store that image away for a moment. Replace it with the very real image—warts and all—of how you see yourself today. Your current skills, relationships, fears, life challenges, and attitudes. How you influence others both positively and negatively. Your character. The person you see in the mirror.

I've never met anyone whose potential and current images are mirror-like identical matches. If you gave yourself a number from 1 to 100, with 100 being your complete, Jesus-breathed potential and your current self as, well, some other number, I wonder what the difference would be.

I'll admit that personally I can see a lot of distance for myself to go. But that doesn't overwhelm me. God loves me as I am right now. He isn't finished with me yet. With His help and grace I can move closer to the goal if I keep at it.

Consider the difference if you increased toward your potential by 10%, 20%, or even 30%. That would be impact everything. If you're like me, it would be life-changing. Isn't that thought worth exploring?

PAUSE & CONSIDER_____

❑ What if everyone on my team
    made that same change?

2.2 DIGGING DEEPER

Before we do anything with your current and potential images, let's unpack them a bit more.

As a Licensed Professional Counselor, my wife Anita often works with clients as they assess an accurate perception of where they are in life. When I shared the contents of this chapter with her, she suggested[7] that considering the following factors may help each of us fill in the picture.

Cognitive factors: Your thinking processes, knowledge, clarity, skill, values, composure, perceptions, interpretation of sensory input, and focus of will.

Intuitive factors: Your emotions, what you sense without necessarily being able to explain, passions, fears, hopes, aspirations, attitudes, creativity, and presuppositions.

Physical factors: Your physical condition, functionality of their senses, comfort, health, age, appearance, weight, height, addictions, exercise, impairments, strengths, endurance, tiredness or restfulness, the impact of the environment, and the physicality of the tools or instruments being used.

---

[7] Thank you, Anita Miller! I have learned so much through your practical insight!

Relational factors: Your interaction and relationship with intimate family, friends, co-laborers, peers, authority figures, church family, and the general public, all within the context of various associated cultural expectations.

Spiritual factors: Understanding your identity in Christ, freedom from spiritual strongholds or sin, maturity in spiritual fruit (love, joy, peace...), the impact of a spiritual walk and disciplines, personal interaction with the Lord, and hearing (and following) the Holy Spirit's leading.

Historical factors: Your background, culture, experiences, triumphs and successes to build upon, and scars from past wounds that continue to impact self-image and ability to move forward.

Current Life factors: Your responsibilities, current skill set, gifts, abilities, training, situation, and resources (gear, finances, time, etc.).

And one final factor before completing these images: no excuses are allowed! Good intentions don't count. You may not be responsible for what others have brought to the table, but you are responsible for what you do with it. Own your images.

Alright! Here comes the big question.

PAUSE & CONSIDER_____

❏   Having considered all these factors,
     how do these two images compare?

The goal of comparison is not to beat ourselves up. A realistic assessment simply helps enable personal growth. It gives us a reference point from which we plot a course and measure improvement.

Understanding our "life factors" allows us to celebrate that the Lord used everything in our life to reach this arrival point, and then move toward the next.

Perhaps you have experienced tragic struggles or have made choices with negative consequences. You may even fear that they hinder your ability to reach your potential.

You may have some very real roadblocks that require addressing. Thankfully, the Lord is the ultimately creative problem solver. Countless times He's overcome situations like bondage, abuse, fear, addiction, damage, pain, separation, and even death. And He wants the absolute best for you!

I'm discovering that I make better choices when I keep my potential image in the forefront of my mind. After all, that's who I want to be. I realize that God's plans and perspective may eclipse my own. My dreams of the future have been at times overly aggrandized or passively underwhelming. Prematurely discovering the image He holds for me may petrify me; it's too big for my brain. Even so, my limited version points me in the right direction as I step more deeply into what it means to be the person God anointed me to be.

2.3 MEET WITH THE MASTER

I realize that comparing images and working toward a goal cannot substitute following the Master's voice. But learning to become more intimate with Jesus allows us access to Him as our guide, the true Author and Finisher of all we can become. Before you fully form your plans for growth, consider first sharing your images with Him.

You may even experience a bit of fear. What if He rejects your image or changes it to something outside of your control? Or worse yet, what if He declares that you are reaching too high for who you really are, that your hopes are out of reach, and that you are irreparably flawed and worthless?

It may be hard to believe—I mean *deep-down* believe—that He truly is greater than any fear or doubt. But He is.

If you face such fears, I gently suggest that you give Him your current and potential images all the same. Trust that He—above all others—senses your desires, secret fears, dreams, and aspirations. He knows your heart better than you do yourself. He knows your images better, too. You are safest, strongest, *best* in His hands.

A college friend confided one morning she was unsure how to be intimate with Jesus. She hungered for the change that she knew personally encountering Him would bring. She desperately needed that impact. She decided to literally go into her closet with her Bible and a journal, then wait. Even though she feared that He may not show up, she committed to not emerge until she felt the Lord's presence.

I didn't see her until that evening. Her face beamed. I had never before seen her smile so radiantly. Meeting Him changed everything.

You can trust Him with your Now and your Wow.

Eric Good, a worship leader from whom I have learned much and have been challenged by many times, shared this thought with me:

> **"Paying attention to personal development and growth journey is so key; unless it happens regularly and at profound levels, we just live in empty shells and our service and ministry lack real depth."[8]**

Allow Jesus to shape your current and potential images. Regardless of the method you use to connect with Him, whether journaling, contemplating scripture, praying with a friend, walking in the woods, or running, (I play guitar in my studio or stand in the ocean waves), simply lay your plans before the Lord and wait.

Numerous times in my life I found it helpful to get away and simply be alone with the Lord. Such times often preceded major life decisions, including deciding to focus my life on ministry, getting engaged, leaving teaching to start a company, and writing this book.

For example, I wrestled with the idea of leaving my advertising agency to step into a full time worship position. I needed God's confirmation. Anita and I took two days off on our own—I settled into a secluded cabin at a silent retreat center (The Hermitage) armed with a notebook, a loaf of bread, water, and a big chunk of feta cheese. She stayed at our house, spending time biking and hiking the paths near the channel dam. Afterwards, we came together to share

---

[8] Eric, your heart for the Lord has always blessed and challenged me. You led one of my favorite highlight-reel moments in worship ever. Thank you!

what we sensed. We were on the same page. We had our answer. Our commitment solidified. God showed us who we were to become, and then together we took the plunge. It resulted in a major turning point in our lives that ultimately impacted many people.

You may find time away to be helpful for you as well. Sometimes growth remains elusive until we create space, a *pause* during which our transformation can unfold. That's similar to one of the purposes for a worship set: to create a moment in which we each encounter and respond to God. Finding that pause in your own life is a way of getting off your mat to move forward. It allows you time to distinguish between your own ideas and the Lord's voice.

How does one grow character? Keep a teachable heart and continually listen for the Lord's prompting whisper. Jesus sent you the Holy Spirit to teach and guide you. Listen.

Follow His nudge.

PAUSE & CONSIDER_____

❑   When I envision the best location for allowing myself the distance necessary to clarify my perspective, what do I think the Lord may say to me there?

2.4 HOW TO DEVELOP CHARACTER

Ultimately, God develops your character. So should we lock ourselves in our own closets waiting indefinitely for some mystical vision or supernatural encounter?

Part of growing character has to do with *remaining*. After talking about boasting in confidence we have of God's ability to transform us, the Bible says in Romans 5:3-4:

"Not only so, but we also glory in our sufferings, because we know that suffering produces perseverance; perseverance, character; and character, hope."

Rather than sequestering ourselves in a corner removed from struggle or action, it seems that Paul writing here that we should stay the course and embrace difficult situations. We don't hide. We sacrifice and suffer. Character is one of the results.

We already noted from Ephesians 4:11-16 that the Lord didn't leave us to flounder around guessing how to mature. He provides us with leaders charged to equip us to serve. We cannot serve casually. In the context of serving we grow and mature to attain the "whole measure of the fullness of Christ."

Serving provides us an environment in which we can grow.

Usually it seems that developing character means getting to our feet to keep moving on in the midst of our situation.

I think the Lord delights when we get off our mat to begin walking and partnering with Him. Time after time in the scriptures, you can discover the importance of a person's willingness to take action. The same is true today.

Moving forward in faith can be the catalyst that precedes your miracle of transformation.

I want to share with you a practical exercise that has truly born fruit in my own life. It helps me avoid passively waiting for growth to occur. I combine daily time talking with God and some form of personal Bible study with this Character Challenge.

The 5-step character challenge

1. Take several days to understand in detail who the Lord says I am, my true Kingdom identity, person I was created to be.

2. Realistically recognize my actions, fears, thoughts, reactions, and behaviors. Consider what they reveal about the how I view myself. Take several days to honestly clarify the image of my potential self.

3. Take several days to identify the key differences between the current and potential me. Address sin issues first.

4. Seek the Lord's guidance as you create a measurable action plan. Spend several weeks working daily to accomplish your plan. At the end of that time, evaluate what you learned.

5. Rinse and repeat!

It's really all about being committed to deliberate growth.

In *Think and Grow Rich*[9]—arguably one of the most influential books on leadership written since the industrial revolution—

---

[9] Thank you, Paul Martinelli, for introducing this book to me and insisting that I hold my image!

Napoleon Hill identified four absolutely necessary ingredients for a person to persist in growth:

1. A definite purpose backed by a burning desire for its fulfillment

2. A definite plan, expressed by continuous action

3. A mind closed tightly against all negative and discouraging influences

4. A friendly alliance with one or more persons who will encourage you on to follow through with both plan and purpose[10]

You can see how each of these ingredients helps align a person toward growth. They streamline one's focus. They eliminate distractions.

You may find yourself more naturally inclined toward some of them, and others may present a greater challenge.

My independent nature makes ingredient number four the hardest for me, but it has born fantastic fruit in my life, including the book you now hold in your hands.

Perhaps that's because I'm learning that involving other people who are invested in my growth really do provide powerful assistance through prayer, accountability, and encouragement. [11] They help me be honest in my assessments. You may find that involving others increases your results, too.

In counseling terms, the word "resilience" refers to your ability to grow and handle difficulty. Incorporating other people is one of the greatest ways to help you go the distance. Plus, you're providing a golden opportunity to serve in a very practical and significant way: partnering with Jesus and you to help in your next step of growth.

Why withhold that opportunity?

---

[10] Napoleon Hill. *Think and Grow Rich*. New York: Fawcett Books, 1987.

[11] Thank you, Thinking Partners! (See *Acknowledgement* section)

BORN FOR WORSHIP

❑ How can I incorporate other people as
I take one practical, measurable step
to move from my Now to my Wow?

2.5 TRANSFORMATION STEALERS

Anyone serving in ministry knows that sometimes unexpected things come up. Life happens. Surprises compete with focusing on growth. We all face transformation stealers such as busyness.

Having too much on my plate can be a big transformation stealer. I'm lured by a false sense of responsibility. I love brainstorming, and have many ideas about all that can be accomplished. I think "I can do all that." But giving in to this temptation leads to my assumption that I have to be the person to get it all done; I forget that adding the task to my plate means I've taken it off someone else's and disabled their opportunity to serve. Then, before long, my to-do list may become paralyzing.

Just as devastatingly, transformation stealers insulate us from the heart of God.

For me, one of the greatest transformation stealers that I face has everything to do with my role in worship.

True worship flows out of a head and heart which is aligned 24-7 with God without distraction. Much of what we do in worship-arts ministry is connected with creating worship expressions. Expressions of worship are just that—external responses that result from our interacting internally with God. Without that internal interaction, expressions themselves, even if artful, are meaningless.

The act of crafting worship expressions can in itself become a transformation stealer. I continually discover that I'm not the only one who experiences this.

Consider all that you pour into your ministry role. For many of us, our worship expression is closely related to our sense of identity and how we encounter the Lord. We must pay attention to all of that because—even more than being our role—it's the avenue through which we express our souls; it is our spiritual voice. It's not surprising that we sometimes cross the little gray divide between focusing on God Himself and focusing on our *method* of connecting with Him.

That's when we allow a shift in one of the major avenues God uses to create transformation in us. It changes from asset to obstacle.

We worship-arts musicians, technicians, and artists sometimes forget that giving God the gift of our whole selves as our reasonable sacrifice includes laying onto His altar our most meaningful expressions of worship. We confuse *expression* with *worship*.

God values the unreserved gift of our heart *far greater than the* noise we make.

The heart determines the expression's value, not what we judge as the expression's actual artistic merit. While being on stage or behind the equipment allows us to impact others with our gifts, expressing true worship to God requires neither a stage nor an audience.

God wants to walk with us. We can embrace His conversation, or we get caught up in making music. I know the choice that I want to make. But all the details of my role sometimes feels overwhelming.

I think it was Ivan Misner who supplied my solution. He's an incredibly productive person himself. He founded Business Network International (BNI), and was dubbed "The Father of Modern Networking" by CNN. He suggested that I list out all my primary responsibilities, and identify whether or not I was required to either personally complete them or verify that they were completed. Then we prioritized the overall importance to my role of each of those primary responsibilities. We discovered that instead of taking up my entire time with all of these tasks, I was able to hand many of them on to others and free myself for the truly important things.

People who serve tend to be asked to serve more. It's so easy to become task-bound. Whether a role or other responsibilities we face, we each address our own collection of transformation stealers.

PAUSE & CONSIDER_____

❑   How can I address my primary
     transformation stealer?

I'm reminded once again of a phrase I heard regularly from Bob Cook[12], the Executive Pastor at a church where I served as Worship Pastor. I've found myself using his statement regularly. He said (to staff and volunteers alike), "You are the steward of your own life."

When I'm thinking about developing character, I realize that Pastor Bob hit the nail squarely on the head. So every day I make a deliberate good choice that aligns my character a little more closely with the person God created me to be.

You can make the good choice, too. Your character sets the pace for everything else you do and become. It provides the foundation upon all you build. It guards your long-term impact. And you have the unique opportunity to embrace developing your character in everything you encounter. Guard your character. Allow God to guide your growth as you remain on His training path, even when your knees get skinned, you grow weary, and the journey requires more sacrifice than it is convenient to give.

Grow your character every day. You will grow it well.

_____

[12] Thank you, Bob for your practical and disciplined approach to discipleship.

2.6 CONSIDER THAT YOU ARE CALLED

My wife is a Chicago Cubs fan from a family of diehards. In her favorite dream, she is an usher at Wrigley Field. During her growing up years she could recite the stats of every player on the roster. Even when pitching her college women's fastball team to nationals, as she took the mound, her mind's eye envisioned herself wearing a Cubs uniform. It's in her blood.

You could tell that her family were Cubs fans. There could be no doubt. Cubs paraphernalia was displayed on the refrigerator, on their clothing, around the house, on the cars, in the workshop, in the greenhouse, along the sidewalk, on TV. It was a part of their free time. It invaded their conversations. Her dad carried 3" x 5" note cards in his shirt pocket on which he'd compile stats for players traded away, all so he could be ready to tell anyone why the manager should have kept them on the team. I don't know how many times my wife's family drove the several hour trek to take in a game, and I certainly had to become accustomed to their stopping anytime, anywhere, to address any perfect stranger wearing a Cubs hat or shirt, and say, "Hey, another Cubs fan!" and begin a conversation.

For me, having been raised in a family where sports didn't play a major role, her family's focus took a bit of adjustment. She took me to my first major league baseball game—Cubs, of course.

The year that the Cubs finally won the World Series, I remember vividly the image of her family hoisting up her father, dressed in full Cubs uniform, and carrying him around the room in celebration. I couldn't help but share some of the contagious enthusiasm.

Here's the point. You never questioned their commitment.

Knowing that the Lord has called you to serve through music and tech should be like that too, don't you think? That strong, that embraced, that contagious?

For me, it's liberating.

Yet how often have you noticed a sense of hesitation in someone on the platform or in a tech booth? Perhaps it's posture or facial expression. Something suggests the tiniest lack of commitment to a note or making just the right sound level change. There's just a subtle nuance hinting, "I don't know if I am really all in."

Maybe you've felt this lack of confidence at some point within yourself. It's a fairly safe bet to suggest that we all have wrestled with that whisper. The nagging, lingering question steals our confidence and pulls our hand back from digging deeper.

Yet it is in that wondrous, frightening, reaching place where much of our greatest transformation awaits.

PAUSE & CONSIDER_____

❑   What in my behavior or attitude limits
     fulfilling my sense of call?

Summoning strength

Knowing one's call frees a person to eliminate encumbrances. It enables setting aside things and activities which don't move toward fulfilling God's call. It frees a person to exchange distraction for determination. That brings exciting, significant results.

Not long after I first began leading a worship team at church, someone anonymously paid for my entrance ticket to attend a worship conference. Conferences were a big deal during those early days of the contemporary worship, and opportunities were rare. I could never have afforded the ticket; it took everything I had just to miss work and buy enough gas for the 6-hour drive. But my wife sent along a couple of apples and I slept in my van in the conference parking lot. I cleaned up in the bathroom each morning before the crowd arrived so I wouldn't smell. How would you feel doing that? For me it was uncomfortable and embarrassing.

But I loved every awesome moment!

Not only did I experience some great worship, but the event stretched and motivated me. I learned foundational concepts I've been building upon for decades. I went because I was convicted that the Lord wanted me to better serve in worship, and the generosity of that anonymous individual fortified my resolve.

In ministry you need the strength that comes from knowing that you're the right person in the right place at the right time—that the Lord is behind all this. His call on your life acts as a permission promising that if you step out, He will complete what He started.

You may call it drive, confidence, vision, or commitment, but whatever IT is, the KNOWING helps us march on in the face of struggle and sacrifice.

Answering any call that the Lord has on your life is a lifelong task; you never "arrive." There's always something new to learn, some new challenge to face, new hurdle to overcome, new technique or tool to master, new technology to understand, new relationship to cultivate. Let's face it, sometimes we tire of *new*. But we all know that true growth—anything worth learning—comes at a price.

The cost of serving in worship-arts ministry cuts deeply. Consider the hours in preparation and team rehearsals, being apart from family during services, dealing with under-appreciation. We face church politics and worship wars. We spend. We take time off work or from family to attend a class or read a book. We modify vacations to visit other churches or attend conferences looking for "one more tip" to make us more effective. We rise early to set up gear. We volunteer or work bi-vocationally because even if the church can pay something, it usually falls far short of supporting a family. Then there are the countless hours spent honing individual skill....

You know what it costs yourself.

Having a sense of call gives one the strength to sacrifice at the level needed to gain the harvest of fruit that the Lord wants to cultivate. Consider your heart to be the soil. The Lord tills it through service, softening it, working it, pulling out weeds, roots, and embedded rocks. He plants a seed—your call. Sacrifice is like a spiritual nutrient which the Lord uses to grow fruit that impacts you and those around on real—and even eternal—levels.

> *Knowing one's call supplies the commitment necessary to remain in the crucible of service.*

That sense of call is one of the greatest motivators the Lord gives. And we worship folk need motivators, don't we? Isn't it a breath of fresh air when something helps us pass through tough times? What we demand from ourselves can be draining.

It's not too farfetched that someone looking in from the outside might think we're a bit crazy for doing what we do.

Knowing one's call allows a person to focus energy on the right things. It supercharges you. It gives you permission to be fanatical.

PAUSE & CONSIDER_____

❑ How would my choices change if I unconditionally, wholeheartedly embraced my sense of call?

2.7 NOT FOR THE FAINT HEARTED

If you've experienced a sense of call on your life, you're in good company. The Bible is full of those who radically embraced the Lord's assignment. Gideon. Esther. Moses. Noah. David. Ruth. The disciples. Even Balaam's mule understood the Lord's direction.

Most of the people who shape the Kingdom and shake the world have an acute sense of God's call.

The apostle Paul had a well-earned reputation for being over-the-top gung-ho. He said in Hebrews 12:1-2,11:

"Therefore, since we are surrounded by such a great cloud of witnesses, let us throw off everything that hinders and the sin that so easily entangles. And let us run with perseverance the race marked out for us, fixing our eyes on Jesus, the pioneer and perfecter of faith. No discipline seems pleasant at the time, but painful. Later on, however, it produces a harvest of righteousness and peace for those who have been trained by it."

He echoed these thoughts in 1 Corinthians 9:24-27:

"Do you not know that in a race all the runners run, but only one gets

the prize? Run in such a way as to get the prize. Everyone who competes in the games goes into strict training. They do it to get a crown that will not last, but we do it to get a crown that will last forever. Therefore I do not run like someone running aimlessly; I do not fight like a boxer beating the air. No, I strike a blow to my body and make it my slave so that after I have preached to others, I myself will not be disqualified for the prize."

Paul's point was simple: drop the dead weight. He was committed. He considered expendable anything that did not directly move toward fulfilling the mission. He didn't look at a call as an inconvenience or even as a responsibility. He looked at a call as *The One Thing*. Everything else was a hindrance to be discarded.

Paul was not talking about quitting your job, divorcing your spouse, throwing your kids out on the street, and living under someone's carport while you practice blues scales on a guitar that you maxed out your credit card to purchase, and "doing ministry."

He does talk about setting aside even good things that capture your time and attention instead of devoting that time and attention toward your call. Not only should a person know their call, but that knowledge should directly impact everything else in their life. Their behavior declares that they are committed and they know it.

Can such an intense sense of call actually interfere with life? Certainly. How could it not? And sometimes every fiber in our being fights against making such Spartan-like choices.

Consider Jonah. His call was perfectly clear. Go tell the people of Nineveh to repent. But Jonah didn't want the people of Nineveh to repent. He didn't want God to let them off the hook for the terribly evil deeds they prided themselves in committing. So Jonah deliberately went to great lengths to avoid God's call, beginning with boarding a boat heading the opposite direction.

Amazingly, God seemed unbothered by Jonah's stubborn rebellion. God just raised the stakes and gave another opportunity to obey. And, sure enough, Jonah eventually did what the Lord wanted, kicking and whining every step of the way. (I have had worship musicians like that!) Jonah preached, the Ninevites repented, and

God delayed the coming consequences for their sin. Jonah complained that the Ninevites should have gotten what was coming to them. And through it all God repeatedly tried offering Jonah opportunities to "get it"—to learn and obey.

What's the big deal? God created fruit through Jonah even though Jonah never seemed to completely embrace his call. A whole nation turned to the Lord and was spared the coming consequences of their sin. I wonder what would have been the increased fruit had Jonah actually run with his call.

PAUSE & CONSIDER_____

❑ What voices in our culture fight against a
   life led by a strong sense of call?

_____

My sense of call is what wakes me at night. Not the fear of making a mistake or facing a tough crowd. I have a sense of excitement. I get wound up with a new idea, hearing a new texture of tones or musical parts in my head, resolving a mastering issue, or phrasing a key workshop point. It's a bit embarrassing to share, but I sometimes wake from a dream exhorting a worshiping congregation as we step deeper into experiencing the Lord. (I wish I could be as eloquent as in my dreams! Who is that guy? Do you do that?) Even typing these words, I'm hitting the keys harder and faster. I'm worked up!

2.8 WAITING FOR THE CALL

Besides character, the next great enabler in our toolbox is a sense of call. It unleashes one's character to tackle a task. But what if a person doesn't experience that strong sense of call? What if it fades when the real work begins?

It stands to reason that at some point everyone questions their sense of call.

When you consider the amount of personal resources consumed by serving in ministry, wrestling through the question of call is extremely important. We wouldn't want to get it wrong.

Probably many of us can think of someone we've known who prematurely assumed an interest, skill, passion, or affirmation from others to be their "holy call." I took that blunder to another level of embarrassment by declaring my misguided plan to others. Then I stepped out in it and <blush!> failed. Miserably. You may have, too.

What if you *are* wrong? It is a legitimate question. But being wrong is a big part of how we learn. Consider humbled pride to be part of the price of the learning curve that eventually leads you to know when you're truly right. Gideon was very afraid of embracing a false sense of call. Even so, after a couple of tests, he committed himself and moved forward irrevocably. I admire that.

Here is something really important that you may want to keep in mind should you not feel like you have a clear sense of call, perhaps even more important than having that giant life purpose statement you can post on the bathroom mirror and in your office.

> *Whether you sense it or not,*
> *the Lord has plans for you.*

There are seasons—sometimes short, sometimes long—that may seem like you are doing nothing but kicking up sand as you hike up and down the sand dunes in the desert of your own heart. Paul waited 2 years following his conversion. Moses spent 40 years in the desert before returning to Egypt when the Lord freed Israel from slavery. Noah was 500 years old and had 3 sons before being directed to build the ark—and the flood didn't come for another 100 years of hard labor. That's a lot of waiting.

Abraham amazes me. He was an important guy, chosen by the Lord to found the nation of Israel. Abraham received God's covenant. I'd assume that God would have spent quite a bit of time with this man. But it didn't work that way.

Of the few times that God actually did personally direct Abraham, it was always unexpected. Abraham would follow the instructions as he saw best, often waiting years until the next interaction. But his commitment to the call from the Lord during these long periods makes him a great example of righteousness.

Sometimes moving forward means you have to wait.

A week before my son Jonathan's due date, our nurse announced that she expected to see us in the hospital delivery room later that very day. We had a room set up as a nursery. Anita's bags were packed. Fresh instructions awaited daily on my desk for a substitute at my classroom where I taught English. Everything was ready to go.

A month later we were still waiting. A full month (31 days = 744 hours = 2,687,400 seconds). Time slowed to a snail's crawl. The chalkboard at school reserved for student and teacher bets of when the baby would arrive had so far surpassed every guessed date and time that no one even glanced at it anymore. Friends and family called so often for updates that we had to change our phone message. "Thanks for calling—no, the baby is *not* here, and yes, this message *is* current. We *will* change it when the baby finally comes. Please do *not* leave a message at the beep!" My wife resigned herself to the fact that she was going to be pregnant forever.

But eventually, to our relief, he was born! We were so excited that we sent out birth announcements. "He's finally here! Introducing Jonathan Robert Miller, 9.3 lbs, 21 inches long. He looks just like his daddy, short, round, and slightly bald!" He was worth the wait.

Your desert time may feel endless, like it drones on and on, but you must persist. You are not doing nothing.

Just the opposite. Even if sensing a lack of *specific* call, you have several bigger life callings to focus upon, set goals for, and engage action plans to accomplish. What can you do? Consider these:

- Grow your character.

- Practice and expand your skill set.

- Get to know Jesus better.

- Address unresolved relational issues.

- Memorize scripture.

- Learn stories of people being impacted that tug at the good things in your heart.

- Move forward in your career.

- Face issues within your culture that you know are important to the Lord.

- Manage finances so that you will be free with resources for when the bigger picture clarifies.

Don't pull to the sidelines and stop. You can be very effective simply by taking your next step for growth in one of these areas. As you develop, you become more and more aligned with the Lord's plan for your life so when the time does come—and it will—you will be ready to move.

Besides, it's often during such time that the Lord is busy working under your level of awareness, developing things you don't even conceive of. Consider that most of the time required for a seed to germinate and grow is spent in the dirt, with no outward sign of growth. He is preparing you for the harvest.

> *Waiting time may actually be your most productive time of all, because waiting time is when much of the groundwork for personal growth occurs.*

These 6 things have help me clarify my sense of call:

- Planting "seeds" through time praying and scripture
- Recognizing what brings me joy
- Removing from my life that which distracts or disqualifies
- Following Romans 12:2
- Interacting with a mature, spiritually aware person as a sounding board or mentor
- Asking for the Holy Spirit's guidance

PAUSE & CONSIDER_____

❑ What encourages me when my sense of call falters?

No sense of call?

Occasionally a willing-and-skilled person volunteers—or is drafted—to fill a church need. Because of that person's servant heart (or guilt complex!), they find themselves on the team. Sometimes beginning to serve this way opens a door to the path of discovering one's real sense of call, and that's awesome!

Still, other times the task remains in the "I'd rather not, but I'm just doing this to help" category.

If you're in an area outside your sweet spot, THANK YOU! Your willingness to step up and faithfully serve moves ministry forward.

There are legitimate, God-honoring reasons to accept the challenges of such roles. Gaps in the church are met. Impact occurs. Filling such roles may encourage and relieve the leader responsible for them. And while you may not prefer the specific job you're doing or serve long-term, you may still find a way to use that task to enable the purpose behind a gift you do have to teach, challenge, organize, encourage, serve, resource, or extend Jesus' love.

Serving is a foundational part of following Jesus. Sometimes it seems like we were custom made to fill a specific role. Other times it feels more like the role chose us instead, and the decision was out of our hands. Every role I've ever filled included some tasks that felt more like a chore than a joy.

But having a sense of call, the inarguable belief that that God Himself has called you—you!—to meet a specific need, that's a fantastic place in which to build, transform, impact, invest, and grow. It's the promise that digging deeply will uncover inconceivable treasure.

That's how Jesus' Bride, the Church, blossoms. Including you.

2.9 CONSIDER YOUR SWEET SPOT

Sometimes it's a tricky challenge to identify a person's actual strengths. I guess it's not surprising, considering the interplay of the elements that connect a person's role with their specific gifts. Things can get clouded because into the mix fall a person's character, the maturity of their spiritual fruit, their various spiritual gifts, their collection of skills and training, the impact of their environment and history, and their personality.

That's quite a stew.

Not only is understanding one's own strengths challenging, so is understanding the strengths of others. But whether serving as a team member or a leader, knowing your ministry partners on cognitive, physical, emotive, and relational levels opens the door for more effective communication.

Many of us do this intuitively with at least some level of success.

Call to mind a couple of your serving partners, people you connect with well. While you may not see eye to eye on everything, there's a good chance that you at least understand one another's values. Your grace for each other helps ease disagreement. Interactions while serving together run more smoothly.

Still, there's more to understanding what drives each of us and makes us tick. It's quite a science. You may be familiar with personality and communication diagnostic tools like the Minnesota Multiphasic Personality Inventory (MMPI), Meyers-Briggs, DISC, CliftonStrengths/StrengthFinder), Four Temperaments, and Game Theory Motivational Assessment. I find them fascinating, and appreciate how each provides its own slice of insight.

When it comes to discipleship and team building, I've learned that communication can be helped by discovering what motivates a person. We're all driven by different values. Realizing each person's motivation allows me to cast vision in ways that each can connect to their own God-given desire for having impact.

Understanding motivations opens our eyes. People who identify their gifts better recognize opportunities to use those gifts. With this knowledge, leaders can position team members to be most effective.

Plus—and this is important—the process of understanding someone else's "why" forces a person to think beyond their own strengths. It helps us willingly share with each other opportunities to be the Lord's tool for harvesting fruit.

It makes sense that the goals of the Church are better reached when more of us operate in our sweet spot.

It's worth taking time to identify gifting accurately. When we mislabel a person's skill set, instead of converting sacrifice into impact, we set up everyone for frustration and disappointment. We waste an incredible bounty of fruit that Lord intended to provide.

Spiritual gifts

Understanding a person's "why" also involves recognizing that person's spiritual gifts.

By the phrase "spiritual gifts" I am not talking about a person's talents, skills, and abilities. I specifically mean the kind of fruit that comes when the Holy Spirit moves through a believer to allow another person to supernaturally experience the touch of God. The result is an increase of the quantity and quality of love, joy, peace, patience, kindness, goodness, gentleness, faithfulness, and self-control.[13] Although spiritual gifts often function hand-in-hand with personality, the two are not the same.

For example, one of my favorite Sunday school teachers had the spiritual gift of teaching. Initially her skill needed training and organization. Thankfully her humor and interesting phrasing kept me engaged. Although I learned something whenever she taught, instead of being something she actually said, I found that the Lord would interrupt my thinking and speak into my life. He would uncover something about myself so that I could move forward. Simply put, I grew. Despite the limitations of her skill, whenever she taught, God consistently worked in my life. That was the incredible fruit of her teaching gift even before she began cultivating her skill set.

Most of us want God to impact uninhibited by limits we bring to the table. To do that, we must operate not only in our talents and training, but—even more importantly—through our spiritual gifts.

That means you and I need to wade through a controversial thicket. Even making a list of spiritual gifts can be doctrinally tricky. Some religious experts clump into their spiritual gift list any Bible keyword following the word "gift," "talent," or even "provision." Other religious experts add skills and personality traits. An entire branch of religious experts discard some gifts that are labeled "spiritual gifts," claiming that these in particular have become irrelevant, inappropriate, or discontinued in our culture or time.

I think that when God says "This is how it works" that this really is how something works. Thank God, I'm not a religious expert!

The Bible says a lot about spiritual gifts. To summarize, the Holy Spirit imparts spiritual gifts to meet specific needs among believers or to impact the unchurched. Here are some things we discover:

---

[13] Galatians 5:22-23

- People find their place in the Church to serve through specific gifts. (Romans 12:3-8)

- Steward and use gifts to honor Jesus. (1 Peter 4:10-11)

- Believers should understand how the Holy Spirit manifests himself through us for the common good, and we should likewise work together in unity. (1 Corinthians 12:1-31)

- God gifts to the Church five roles/positions/offices for the purpose of equipping and growth. (Ephesians 4:7-16)

- We should use our spiritual gifts. (2 Timothy 1:6-7)

- Spiritual gifts help strengthen us. (Romans 1:11)

- Gifts without love have no value. (1 Corinthians 13:2)

- The church needs the full gamut of spiritual gifts. (1 Corinthians 1:3-12)

- Some revelatory gifts will no longer be necessary once we see Jesus face to face. (1 Corinthians 13:8-10)

- We are to desire gifts. (1 Corinthians 14:1)

- The Holy Spirit determines to whom gifts are distributed. (Hebrews 2:4, 1 Corinthians 12:11)

- God's gifts are irrevocable. (Romans 11:29)

- Not all gifts from God fall in the category of spiritual gifts, for example, grace, self-control, love, skill, and scripture. (Ephesians 2:8; Exodus 31:1-6; 2 Timothy 1:7, 3:16-17)

PAUSE & CONSIDER_____

❏ How can exploring and utilizing spiritual gifts in my own life affect how I serve?

2.10 SPIRITUAL MOTIVATIONAL GIFTS

Let's narrow the "explore my tools" conversation from the bigger picture of one's skills, personality, interests, and background.

Romans 12:6-8 lists seven foundational Church-building spiritual gifts. These gifts are described differently than gifts mentioned in other biblical passages. The Lord has placed a gift in every believer to shape how we approach effective ministry. If we truly want to be the best we can be, it makes sense that we take a look.

Think of the seven spiritual gifts listed in Romans 12:6-8 more as SPIRITUAL MOTIVATIONS through which we serve rather than as specific ACTIVITIES or SKILLS used to accomplish our call.

Allow me to clarify that. Think of a simple example of setting up extra chairs for an event. Setting up chairs is not a spiritual gift. But one's Spiritual Motivation helps determine the approach a person takes to accomplish the task and how they evaluate success.

There's nothing particularly glamorous about setting up chairs. We're not going to get interviewed by Worship Leader Magazine.

Most of us don't wake up and jump from the bed exclaiming, "Today is the day I get to set up chairs, hallelujah!" Even so, this example highlights the different pay-offs that motivate people to do the job. It reveals each person's "why."

Let's take a closer look at the Spiritual Motivation gifts. See which one best describes how you approach serving.

The *prophetic motivation* desires that people understand and obey what God is saying. Setting up the chairs is a necessary means to that end. The action creates a kind of a living picture of their faithful belief that the Lord will bring someone to fill those seats. They pray that the Lord's message will be heard and that people will respond. They desire that sinful bonds will be broken, and that people will turn more closely to the Lord.

The *organizing motivation* desires that people are able to fulfill their tasks, that events run smoothly, and that the goals of events are accomplished. While setting up chairs according to organized plan is a means to that end, this person is also most likely to ask someone else to help.

The *exhorting motivation* desires that people understand the steps they need to know in order to move forward, and to have hope that things will be OK. While setting up the chairs may be a way to communicate encouraging appreciation to the person in charge of the event or to help the event take place, the exhorter may become distracted or do a quick and somewhat less tidy arrangement before moving on to something more interesting. But if there's a way to have fun setting up chairs, this person will find it.

The *teaching motivation* desires that people learn truths. So it matters to this person that the chairs are set up in a way that enables people to see the primary person speaking and the content on a screen, and to be able to take notes and retain the information.

The *serving motivation* desires that tasks are completed because doing so fulfills a need in and of itself. "Get 'er done." The chairs will be set up quickly, with attention to detail. Satisfaction comes from completing the job. This person doesn't prefer to draw extra attention to themselves, and may struggle the most if someone else comes along and rearranges the chairs or sits in them prematurely.

The *giving motivation* desires to see resources (time, energy, finances...) used effectively for Kingdom purposes. This person may pay attention to the condition of the chairs and that they are the appropriate chairs for the needs of that event. Wobbly legs, gum under the seats, or vandalized cushions would particularly bother this person.

The *mercy motivation* desires people to feel Jesus' love. This person may be thinking about or praying for those who will fill the seats, or may enjoy the task more if there's someone else to talk with. This person may also deviate from the planned setup to help people more comfortably connect with each other.

What in this list feels familiar?

PAUSE & CONSIDER_____

❑   How could people who know and
     value me help distinguish the difference
     between my skills/personality and my
     Spiritual Motivation gift?

2.11 HONORING OUR GIFTS

Sometimes we struggle over and over with the task to which God calls us. Maybe the scope feels overwhelming. Maybe we've just blown it or put it away so long that it seems a forgotten dream.

Moses is an interesting example. He initially had to flee for his life after attempting prematurely to take on the issue. Then, after 40 years of sheep herding in exile, when God reminded him of his call, he tried to pass it to his brother Aaron.

When Moses acted out in his frustration, significant consequences usually followed. Still, we must give him credit for taking on what is arguably one of the most difficult tasks in human history. The people of Israel did arrive at the promised land, where they were continued to be led by the person Moses hand-picked and prepared to take up his mantle once he was gone. Moses' connection with God was incredible. My point is that even Moses sometimes struggled with his attitude about the gifts and callings from God.

> *It's no surprise that when there is no direct association between a task and a person's Spiritual Motivation gift, frustration and discouragement usually result.*

Sometimes we inconsistently weigh the value of the different

Spiritual Motivation gifts. We may find one more appealing than another. I suppose that's why the Romans 12:6-8 passage packages the gifts content between a verse on humility and a whole section about love. Perhaps we consider our own Spiritual Motivation gift inherently superior to the rest, and lack tolerance for how other people approach serving. If allowed, these attitudes lead to an imbalance of fruit and focus in the Church Body.

People sometimes even devalue their own fruitfulness. Here's an important example I experienced when someone refused to consider his own Spiritual Motivation gift worthwhile.

Rick was born and bred to be a pastor. His father was a pastor. His brothers were pastors. Rick invested himself in preparing to become a pastor, too. He earned a Bible degree in college and completed seminary. He presented himself as an exhorter, a teacher, and an organizer. And sure enough, he was hired to pastor a small congregation. But it didn't last.

In spite of Rick's passion and training, his gifts simply didn't align with his desires.

It wasn't that Rick wasn't gifted. He was. I experienced firsthand the fruit of his true Spiritual Motivation gifts of Serving and Giving. Good fruit always resulted. But he didn't want to use them. He felt that different gifts were better suited for the pastorate. So he relied on his energy and intellect to manufacture the kind of fruit that only truly remains when delivered through Spiritual Motivation gifts.

> *Well-intentioned human effort and skill, regardless of its quality and the sacrifice spent on it, cannot cultivate the fruit that results from a Spiritual Motivation gift. It simply doesn't work.*

So as Rick completed the pastoral tasks, the fruit just wasn't there.

When a person withholds from serving through their Spiritual Motivation gift, the potential fruit that others receive becomes stilted. The personal growth that should be experienced by the person serving doesn't happen. The progress of spiritually maturing grinds to a halt.

It's not surprising that someone expending so much energy and time could become frustrated and disillusioned when their investment lacks the returns they had envisioned.

It makes sense that such a conflict would lead a person to become bitter and resentful. You'd expect from them more whining and complaining than joy and patience. And because they sense their failure—whether consciously or not—it builds up and spills out to flavor relationships and business. It builds walls. It harms. And it insulates a person from experiencing the kind of impact that God created them to have upon others.

That's the sad story of Rick.

But we don't need to live that way.

The Bible clearly states that all gifts are valuable, honor Jesus, produce important fruit, and are needed by the Church. Embracing Spiritual Motivation gifts places us in directly in the front and center of the Lord's design for having lasting impact.

By identifying the Kingdom-building Spiritual Motivation which your role allows you to fulfill, even a task as basic as setting up extra chairs provides you opportunity to accomplish something valuable. Jesus uses gifts as a pipeline to supply His love to the world. Through your gift you extend Jesus' touch.

PAUSE & CONSIDER_____

❑ How can I help encourage someone having
    a different Spiritual Motivation gift than
    mine and help them realize their value?

2.12 SPIRITUAL MOTIVATIONS COLLIDE

Working well together is easier when you understand one another's personality and communication style. Knowing how everyone's Spiritual Motivations interact can smooth navigating the conflicts that naturally arise when serving. And you know that conflict happens.

Consider this scenario. Someone loses their job. The responses that person receives will vary significantly as influenced by the respondent's Spiritual Motivation gift.

- A *prophetic motivation* response may focus on how God is addressing the person's need for repentance or change. The job loss may be seen as a consequence of sin or as a wake-up call to walk more closely with the Lord.

- An *organizing motivation* response may focus on understanding the factors contributing to the job loss, and to the connections or resources available that may point to a new job that may be a better fit for that person.

- An *exhorting motivation* response may focus on cheering up the person. Specific steps may be offered to address the situation. The conversation would renew hope and provide the knowledge of what to do next.

- A *teaching motivation* response focuses on clarifying

details and understanding what the person could learn through the experience. The teacher may share stories of how others facing similar situations are examples to follow, or explain résumés and Indeed.com jobs postings.

- A *serving motivation* response may focus on finding out how the person may need practical assistance as they move forward such as meals, childcare, or transpiration that would enable the urgent job search process.

- A *giving motivation* response may focus on addressing resources impacted by the job loss, and also on resources available to help the person address the situation (money, time, energy, relational connections, supplies, etc.).

- A *mercy motivation* response may focus on the person's feelings and communicate compassion for those involved. By the end of the conversation there would be a sense that the person is cared for.

Each approach cares for different aspect of a person's life. Still, those offering help may think that other viewpoints miss what "really matters." The mercy person may take offense to the teaching person's apparent insensitivity. The Serving person may think the Exhorter's lighthearted perspective to be overly impractical and fluffy. The Prophetical person may think the Giving person prematurely bails out the person before full internal personal or spiritual change occurs.

Each person views ministry through the lens of their Spiritual Motivation gift. Each thinks, "No one cares like I do." And they're right. Each gift offers its own distinct and vital brand of care.

A person may need to receive from the different Motivational Gifts at different stages of an experience. We're far ahead by honoring and allowing room for the full range of Spiritual Motivation gifts even when we believe that our approach is best. Such attitude arises from maturing in the fruit of God's Spirit.

❏ How does my Spiritual Motivation gift
    interact with the other ones?

Let's apply this concept to a worship-arts ministry example.

Someone chronically shows up late for practice. This bothers other team members, and their mood sours. The feeling in the room becomes increasingly heavy. One person tries a joke to lighten things before the downward spiral gets out of hand. Some musicians simply shut down. Others comment about the need to be prepared. People feel like they're walking on egg shells. Practice loses its sense of joy and excitement, and becomes an endurance challenge.

Sound familiar?

How might a person of each of the Spiritual Motivation gifts be impacted by a person's chronic tardiness? How could tardiness affect another person's ability to function in their gift? What frustrating message is inadvertently communicated? How can one person use their Spiritual Motivation gift to restoratively address the problem?

❏ When I think of a potential conflict that
    might arise while serving, how could people
    of differing Spiritual Motivation gifts join
    together to better address it?

It makes sense. Conflicting roles and competing values birth conflict. Working with music draws from very personal areas in us, and we can attach blindly to our own perspectives. Besides, we work with demanding time constraints, cramped sonic quarters (volume wars, anyone!), and lots of expensive gear in tiny physical areas.

When the *something* that deeply matters to each of us collides with another person's agenda, it's like poking a nest of hornets.

Add to this the fact that we're targeted by an evil adversary who delights in attempting to defile anything marked to glorify the Lord. Grace helps overcome conflict which could otherwise fuel the enemy's schemes. It can disarm offenses and irritations coming from leaders over you, your co-laborers, and those you serve.

So what do you do when Spiritual Motivation gifts collide? Hide and ride out the storm? Pray it works out and allow the loudest voice to win? Fight for your view?

Here are 3 keys:

1. **Have grace.** Extending grace means pausing to remember that there's always a bigger picture. By responding to one another with the patience and love of Jesus, we allow Him to do His work. There's a reason Spiritual Motivation gifts are sometimes called "Grace Gifts."

2. **Respect the Leader's role.** Before jumping in to resolve an issue or align everyone to your viewpoint, consider that it may be more appropriate for your leader to address the situation, especially if already present. If you are the leader, lead.

3. **Communicate carefully**. Sometimes it's best to address the elephant in the room. Rather than escalating the issue or venting, stick with team values and the consequential impact of the issue upon yourself. Take responsibility for your part.

Consider this possible response to the tardy issue. *"I'm hoping to communicate where I'm coming from. I try really hard to honor the Lord by respecting everyone's time. So I prepare my part before we rehearse. I get here early enough to be set up, ready to play at our start time. I feel discouraged when you come late because it feels like my offering to the Lord was wasted. I struggle with that attitude. Can you help me?"*

My friend Jerry Hershberger explains his approach learned through 30 years of playing on worship teams. "I need to humble myself whenever the sinful 'I'm always right' attitude creeps in. Too often I'm overly quick to judge. Grace and patience should be at the forefront of how I deal with people. How much grace and patience has God given me? I still make mistakes. Yes, issues may need addressing, but we need grace as God would give it."[14]

---

[14] Jerry, perhaps you learned grace from dealing with serving on teams with me! You're an awesome bass player and an encouraging confidante.

❏ How can understanding a person's Spiritual Motivation Gift help me extend grace to my teammates, leaders, and the people I'm trying to impact?

2.13 TRANSFORMATION, GIFTS, AND UNITY

Working with other people in worship-arts ministry is not always easy. Let's face it, we're artists!

Even if everyone on you team is the best of friends, you'll still experience disagreements. People let us down. And if the Church is a place where God draws together people on a path of transformation, it shouldn't be overly surprising that people "in development" may cause frustration and even pain. Sheep butt heads.

Sometimes God's opportunity to focus your attention on an area needing personal growth comes in the form of conflict amongst those very "dear brothers and sisters in Christ" with whom you serve. It amazes me how quickly my own stubbornness can rise to the surface when I work with another person who is just as headstrong! Lord, have mercy!

Yet in or around so many of the Bible's passages about transformation, growth, and using one's gifts, there's usually something also mentioned about the Church growing in unity.

Perhaps that's a reason why relationships in worship-arts ministry are so challenging. Just like in marriage, interactions with one another create the friction that allows areas within you to rise up to your attention—and perhaps everyone else's—to alert your radar that you face an opportunity (and need) for transformation.

When I grow, when you grow, we both become more aligned with Jesus' attitudes. We mature. The fruit of the Holy Spirit increases in our lives, meaning that we have more good stuff in us necessary for relational bridge building. This fruit helps us handle some of the rough bits in each other that have not yet been smoothed out. The Church grows in quality and character. Growth directly links serving with building unity.

My brother says it this way, "It's like we're all coffee beans; we're all a bit different, but the blend is good."[15]

Perhaps that's why God designed the best context for our own growth to be in situations when we're around other people.

Some of us thrive around with other people. If that's you, then people probably energize you. Being with others provides you with a sense of fun and excitement or with a sense of relational connection. Whether you prefer being with a small, intimate group or with a large, noisy throng, at heart you're a people-person.

Perhaps you're more of an independent person who energizes from time alone. That may be when you make the best plans or complete tasks most efficiently.

I realize that most of us are a blend of these approaches. Even so, wherever we find ourselves on the spectrum, we sometimes have trouble understanding and legitimizing those who feel differently. Our answer to the "Can't we all just get along?" should be a resounding "Yes!" When it's not, we each have something to learn.

Whichever your preference, your walk with the Lord includes your role in the Body of Christ—the Church. Part of your growth and part of the growth of others requires that connection. Jesus designed it that way. Whether you are a people-person or not, your growth

---

[15] Thank you, Todd for your love of coffee analogies!

directly impacts the Kingdom and beautifies Jesus' Bride.

So it is appropriate when we discuss becoming more effective in ministry that we first talk about God's goal for ministry: transformation; His reason for transformation: love; and His context for ministry: serving others.

PAUSE & CONSIDER_____

❑   What can I learn from admitting when I am
     most tempted to allow unity to slip?

2.14 TAGTEAM POWERHOUSE: SPIRITUAL MOTIVATION AND PASSION

There's more to finding one's sweet spot in ministry than identifying gifts and callings. It involves honoring the Lord with the sum total of a person's emotive and cognitive self.

It's sometimes called the fire-in-the-belly. The divine inspiration. The all-consuming obsession. The depths of one's heart (or "bowels" in the ancient Hebrew). The Bible records in Matthew 22:37-38 that Jesus said that loving the Lord with the combination of heart, soul, and mind is our greatest commandment of all.

We'll simply call it *passion*.

Our culture has a love/hate relationship with passion. Blindly following one's passion is a two-edged sword. It can embolden a person to step beyond the comfort zone and achieve great things. But if misdirected, it can lead one into folly and tragedy. It both inspires and frightens us, so we often cautiously hold it at bay.

However, when one's passion becomes focused through the lens of a Spiritual Motivation gift and guided by submission to the Holy Spirit, it's like rocket fuel to ministry.

They are entwined. So let's consider passion.

I often ask people attending my training sessions what most excites them about serving. That's when they become animated and their eyes light up. The pace of their talking quickens and their hand gestures increase. Somewhere, somehow, their sense of duty or call has put feet to what they really care about, to their passion.

A sense of call aligns the passion in your heart because serving in your call moves your toward the life goal of being a co-worker with the Lord. You're made for it. It empowers the special gifts endowed specifically to you by the Lord to make you effective. If you believe in giving your whole self to God, you cannot withhold your passion. You honor Him by doing what He breathed into you to do. It brings both you and the Lord joy.

A sense of calling is the spark;
passion is the fully blossomed fire.

And God wants the passion that He originally sparked in our hearts through a sense of call to blaze even hotter. It's interesting to me that building that fire is our job rather than the Holy Spirit's.

The Bible says in 2 Timothy 1:6:

"For this reason I remind you to fan into flame the gift of God, which is in you through the laying on of my hands."

The passage goes on by stating that operating with a blazing, passionate inner fire has a spirit of power and love and discipline. No weak, little timid fire here.

When I read this verse, I can't help but remember the blacksmith shops in the cowboy movies I watched while growing up, and how the smith would pump the bellows and intensify the fire to a cherry red inferno sending up showers of sparks.

God Himself models passion. The Bible says in Isaiah 42:13:

"The LORD will march out like a champion, like a warrior he will stir

up his zeal; with a shout he will raise the battle cry and will triumph over his enemies."

This is the very image of conquering, overwhelming potency. Pure, unstoppable passion. Woohoo! For me, that's exciting.

Passion drives ministry. It feels like one's life and breath. It compels us to give our very best.

Passion must be expressed, or like a coal removed from the fire, it grows cold and fades. Thankfully, everyone in worship-arts ministry has at least one tool to give voice to their passion. It may be a soundboard, a voice (literally!), an instrument, a computer, a paint brush, or a drum stick. And while a person's *voice* is merely the expression of their true passion, that voice can be crafted and improved to better reflect the heart that it breathes out.

Compare this to the temptation of ignoring one's passion, downplaying the significance of serving the Lord. Our enemy would love for worldly cares and activities to distract us from walking in our calling. Perhaps that's why the Bible in 1 Timothy 4:14 warns us to not neglect our gifts and callings. They're the doorway to a passionate, high-impact, exhilarating, and fulfilling ministry that takes on life in Jesus' sized proportions.

Doesn't a life of passionate, effective ministry sound like a good investment of your time, energy, and resources? We've found it! That's your sweet spot.

PAUSE & CONSIDER_____

❑ How could fanning the flame of my own
passion affect my level of impact?

_____

John Maxwell explained how desire grows into passion.

"It begins with a desire. But more than having a desire, it's giving 100% to that desire... Everyone has desires. But for it to continue to progress to get to this all consuming obsession, you have to follow the trail. You have to stoke the fire. You don't just go from desire to that high level. You have to keep walking in that desire. And what

happens is that the more you work it, the more you want it, the more it grows in you... It doesn't grow automatically.

"Here's the problem. Most people think that all the good character traits they need to be successful, once they have them, they stay with them... They just think 'I was very disciplined last week,' and then they stop. It's like 'What I started should happen automatically,' and nothing happens automatically in my life—it has to be intentional. If you stay intentional with desire, you can get to that peak, but you can't get to that peak without staying focused.

"Life changing principles are only life changing if you manage them. The principle isn't life changing. We overestimate the principles and underestimate the management of those principles. It's the management that gets you to that peak."[16]

It's like my image of the blacksmith. Your role is the furnace. Your passion is the bellows. Your gift is the hammer. Your place of ministry is the anvil. You are the ingot being forged.

Passion helps you stay in the furnace and stand the heat so that when it is time for you to come out, you are purified and transformed into something amazing.

PAUSE & CONSIDER_____

❑ When I consider my sense of passion on a scale of 1-10, where am I? Where is my team? What does that mean?

---

[16] Thank you, John Maxwell, for being such a helpful mentor and sharing this over the phone— it's an honor to be a part of your team!

STOPPING

3.0 THE QUESTION

No one wants to talk about this elephant in the room: time. We're not talking about dividing the hours in your day. We are talking about how long you serve in a role, and when the time comes to stop.

We take ministry seriously, but we don't want to feel stuck. Sometimes God moves us elsewhere or has for us a new focus. Perhaps it's good to momentarily step back to gain new perspective before returning with renewed vigor. Other times simply asking the question reminds us that this isn't the time. But at some point most people wrestle with the topic.

There are good reasons we don't want to think about it.

None of us want to damage the Church. Simply walking away could have significant repercussions on church leadership, our teammates, the congregation, and ourselves. It's serious.

Serving affects us. We all tend to wrestle with associating our sense of value or significance with how we serve. We may fear losing future opportunities. It's hard to say goodbye to what we love doing. Besides, if you serve vocationally, there are financial considerations.

Losing key people can be hard for any leader. Your willingness to invest time reading this book reveals that you take Kingdom work seriously, and that's rare gold for any leader to lose.

Those you serve under may rely on you and would hate to see you go. The absence of any hard-won, experienced volunteer or staff person changes how things are done. The overall fruit of the ministry will change. Replacing you may be difficult. You don't want to disappoint either the leaders you support or the ones you serve.

Besides, if we care for those our ministry impacts, we don't want to leave them hanging. Our service in worship makes us a part of how others approach the Lord. And while we know we're not indispensible, we realize that our choices will affect more than ourselves.

We realize stakes are too high for a conscientious person to flippantly throw in the towel. By considering the impact of our choices on Christ's Bride, such hesitation honors Him.

But how long should a person remain in a role for which they feel no sense of call? Is this simply a lull in your level of passion? Is it a sign of something deeper? Or are you trapped in a ministry role and feel that you can never leave?

You're responsible to manage your resources. That accountability includes stewarding your time and energy. Yes, generally people are capable of more than they realize, but doesn't it seems wise to invest yourself where your productivity is highest? Most of us want our serving to return significant results. That usually happens within one's sweet spot. And once we've finally found that sweet spot, it's hard to set it aside.

PAUSE & CONSIDER_____

❑ What does my willingness—or lack of willingness—to lay down a ministry role say about me?

Even if a person manages to find the magic balance formula enabling them to function at 100% efficiency, sometimes job assignments change. There may be a task elsewhere that the Lord has been preparing them to fill with the skills and experiences learned at the current gig. Someone may need to stretch in a new area. Another person may need to step up in the area that you cover, so you need to make room by switching into more of a mentoring/teaching role or simply finding a new sweet spot and growing yourself. Perhaps the Lord may be preparing you for a change into something better aligned with your Spiritual Motivation gift.

It's easy to declare that we want to be where the Lord wants us. But sometimes it's difficult to discern exactly what He has in mind. How do you know?

As you prayerfully seek the Lord's direction in serving, keep in mind that there is an appropriate time to say, "No." Not to the Lord, (remember Jonah?!), but to church leadership. People who get things done well tend to become go-to people when something new comes along or something has fallen through the cracks. Many of us like to be the kind of person who others can count on when their going gets tough. Even so, the Lord didn't create you to do everything.

For the entire duration of the world, from Adam to the day of Jesus' return—one way or another—every person serving in a ministry position eventually stops.

The only questions are *when* and *how*.

PAUSE & CONSIDER_____

❑ What words best describe my thoughts when I think of stepping away from my current ministry role?

3.1 FAIR QUESTIONS

There are good reasons to consider stepping away from a role. While walking with Jesus means that we become His hands and feet to impact those around us (ministry), reassigning roles can be healthy. The question of change needs to be asked.

Frontrunner

Some roles are less about the role itself and more about preparing the way for the next person called to carry that load. What a gift to the Church, covering a gap temporarily as a front runner. That's what John the Baptist said he was doing by paving the way for the Messiah. When it was time, he willingly decreased so that Jesus could increase. Serving by filling the gap can honor the Lord and give you the opportunity to help another person start serving well. And of course, this begs the question, "Who is the frontrunner for you in your next role?"

A nudge in the right direction

Sometimes those who oversee a church need a nudge before willingly restructuring ministry. Shifting roles from one person to another may renew a sense of effective freshness or adjust direction.

Stepping away from your role may even be God's way of bringing to the church leadership's attention that that role has run its course. It may be hard to admit, but refusing to step away at that point could hamper the church's growth.

Church leaders sometimes hesitate to rock the boat by eliminating traditions or popular activities. With the overloaded plates that many of us keep spinning, we easily become caught up in an intricate maintenance dance in which one misstep could make everything tumble. We work under assumed or real expectations from those in authority over us, serving partners, those under our leadership, peers, ourselves, and even the community. If considering a consequential firestorm for making a volunteer or staff personnel change, often the answer is a resounding, "Not now!" However, the Lord may use a role change to nudge leadership toward needed adjustments.

Housecleaning

You may realize while asking the "Is it time for me to change roles?" question that it is actually time for someone else to go. Another possibility is that there may be team members who, although interested, are not truly willing to invest in moving forward together.

Some church worship workers are actually *hobbyists*. Their skills may be awesome, but their priorities, commitments, or interests conflict with the personal investment necessary to accomplish the goals with the rest of the team. Such individuals may feel a strong attachment for the role, but the will or opportunity to prepare for serving isn't enough to continually get the job done effectively.

> *We have to consider the possibility that by allowing people to serve when they really shouldn't, we actually teach the false belief that serving doesn't really matter.*

Perhaps our reluctance to make personnel changes is a significant reason that the Church seems filled with people who can't quite commit, who participate only when convenient, who give sporadically, or who seem so torn between conflicting interests and responsibilities that true fruitfulness remains evasive. With such lack of drive, how easy is it to weather the struggles we inevitably encounter while serving?

I hadn't realized

I vividly remember my son coming to me after I had stepped away from a long-term high-immersion ministry role. He said, "Dad, I'm glad you're not doing that job anymore. It was killing you." Looking back, I realize he was right. The intensity of a job I loved had insulated me from meeting some basic needs in my life, primarily in the areas of cultivating deep relationships and simply getting enough rest and exercise. But I was so involved that I hadn't even realized these deficiencies. He was right; I may not have survived.

You've likely heard the saying, "He can't see the forest through the trees." However, some ministry roles require us to focus closely upon the individual trees. Probably everyone has experienced being so immersed in one thing that something else slipped by entirely unnoticed or the scope of the larger picture becomes vague.

There may be some significant deficit in your life that changing roles may help address. Your future impact may even depend upon it.

The year before marrying Anita I occasionally cleaned large high-temperature oil tanks. For safety, we worked in pairs. One person entered and scraped the tank, and the partner remained outside ready to remove the other by the harness should the heat overwhelm.

Perhaps there's wisdom in Disney's *Finding Nemo* when Crush asks, "Do you have your Exit Buddy?" Ministry partners could help us explore our own gaps, remain relevant, and identify whether it may be time to move on to something more healthy. They can help us stay healthy right where we are. We all need an Exit Buddy. Do you have yours?

PAUSE & CONSIDER_____

❑ What could be a positive impact from passing my role to another person—upon me, my potential replacement, and the church?

3.2 THE RIGHT TIME?

Simply because a role seems to be a perfect fit for what you are certain is the Lord's call upon your life, that does not necessarily mean that this is the role for you *at this moment in your life.*

Sometimes it may seem like a person's call goes on pause. Consider Moses spending 40 years tending sheep before leading the Israelites to the promised land or Joseph serving as a slave and then as an assistant jailer-in-residence before becoming Pharaoh's second in command over the entire Egyptian empire. The Lord may require some important preparation within you before the time comes to continue.

Such times may feel dormant while the Lord works under your hood, teaches you, or prepares others. That's a healthy and necessary part of the impact cycle. Meanwhile you ready yourself by deepening your skill set, developing significant relationships, or focusing on meeting other needs. It may be that the Lord wants to address some key in your life that is vital to your success ahead.

The first time I experienced one of these difficult pauses occurred following a decade of serving as a worship volunteer. I realized that the Lord was calling me to more involved service, possibly in a full time capacity. I didn't know how to move forward, but the Lord had a plan, part of which unfolded by directing me to begin attending another church for training. Leaving our church family was painful. The following six months passed without my playing a single note on stage. It felt so dry! I continually wrestled with doubts about whether I had heard from Him correctly. But as I remained faithful to the plan I believed He had revealed, He taught me several key leadership truths that I had been missing. What I learned during that down time dramatically improved how I prepared and led teams. I just shake my head when I think of all that I—and everyone serving under me— would have missed without that difficult time of discovery.

You know what? While I played a significant worship role at the church I left in order to learn, now—nearly 20 years later—that congregation still has a vibrant passion for worship, even without me. God cared for them without my help.

Timing is up to the Lord, and we'll be successful if we keep our eyes fixed on where He points while walking to His cadence. The active season will come around again. Embrace the down time; you'll need it for what's coming!

Job for life?

Have you ever run into someone serving in worship-arts ministry who seems to believe that they've carried their role so long and successfully that they own it. They have earned the right to call it theirs in a "You'll have to pry it from my cold, dead fingers" kind of way? You know how such stories inevitably end with lots of prying and lots of dying—at least to self.

One of my early worship mentors cautioned, "Hold ministry loosely, or you'll end up with no ministry and sore fingers."

Performing v.s. facilitating worship

One of the greatest goals of facilitating worship has absolutely nothing to do with making a sound or pushing a button. This goal isn't about your expression of worship at all.

I'm referring to the part of leading that simply provides an opportunity for others to engage by expressing their hearts. This is when we serve best by getting out of the way and directing all focus toward Jesus.

The goal of performing is different, and draws the audience toward one's message, one's skill, or even the shared experience of creating something of artistic merit. There's value in performing. Serious messages can be communicated. Art and thoughtful space is created. Even lighthearted fun and entertainment can fulfill legitimate, valuable, and necessary roles in our culture.

And while similar skills and technologies are used both in leading worship and in performing, worship-arts ministry is not about seeking 5 minutes of glory. It's not *America's Got Talent*. Those experiences are for people who want to perform.

What can a performance-focused musician or technician do if they find themselves helping in worship-arts ministry yet they realize that they're not called to serve the church using that particular skill set?

It's simple. In the best way possible, and as soon as possible, stop.

Maybe that sounds harsh. But think about it. There are plenty of alternative ways to perform and bless others with one's abilities. Assist with the high school musical production. Play in a trio. Join a band. Write. Record advertising jingles. Have a home studio. Build loops. Perform for people who appreciate what you do. Get paid. Have fun. Get on with enjoying what you really are called to do, and leave room for the person actually called to take on this worship job.

Certainly, there's a great place for helping the Church by serving in a role temporarily to fill a gap, but if prolonged too long, frustration usually follows. That's because serving long term outside your call prohibits you from doing what the Lord actually has in mind for you to be partnering on with Him in the first place. Your Spiritual Motivation gift remains unfulfilled.

Somehow one's spirit senses this discrepancy. Even if not consciously realized, resentment begins to build, spilling out in unresolved anger, frustration, dissatisfaction, doubt, or depression. It's the Proverbs 13:12 *"Hope deferred makes the heart sick"* principle that inevitably finds a way to express itself.

Whether a person avoids their call like when Jonah deliberately fled from turning Nineveh toward repentance, or a person's sense of call simply slips away unnoticed because of other concerns, sometimes the Lord must resort to more extreme measures in order to draw attention back and realign one's thinking. I've never found that to be pleasant. It reminds me of Balaam's experience with his donkey, and also of a book called *A Whack On The Side Of The Head*. Ouch! Perhaps you have had a similar experience.

We each need to be doing what the Lord has called us to do.

The saying goes, "No call, you fall."

The fall comes because eventually meeting the needs of ministry through your own strength instead of through the Lord's cannot last. Operating within your call pushes you beyond your own resources into a place requiring the Lord's intervention. He steps in by lavishing an increase in love, strength, patience... whatever is needed for His kind of eternal fruit to be born and flourish. That "lack and filling" process is part of your transformation, your becoming more like Jesus. Ministry apart from your call may even thrive for a while, but true spiritual fruit—the kind that lasts for eternity—is missing.

I'll say it again. No call, you fall. And if your call is elsewhere shouldn't you be, too?

PAUSE & CONSIDER_____

❑   What may be the consequences if I
     refuse to consider setting aside my role
     in worship-arts ministry?

3.3 NEXT STEP FOR THE STUCK

Usually feeling stuck in ministry does not mean stepping away.

Finish well

If the time *has* come to step down from a ministry role and no one rises to replace you, you know the importance of talking with the appropriate leadership. Right away. It's fair and responsible to share with leadership what you're realizing. Together, you may find an alternative approach that better aligns the role with your Spiritual Motivation gift and resources, swap some responsibilities with another person, or create a reasonable endgame plan with appropriate deadlines for you to transition out of that role entirely.

> *If it's time to you to stop, support the ministry and honor the Lord by finishing well.*

Fan the weak flame

If it's *not* time to be done, roll up your sleeves, embrace your call, stir up your passion the fire in your belly—and the Spiritual Motivation gift within you—and get to work!

We both know that solutions are easy to say and tough to obey.

Faltering ministry could be a sign of burnout or facing ministry challenge. Carey Nieuwhof's book *Didn't See It Coming*[17] provides great insight into overcoming what he refers to as the 7 greatest challenges that no one expects and everyone experiences. If you suspect that running out of steam for ministry is a symptom of something significant inside, taking a couple of days to consider the observations he shares may be the best medicine you're going to find.

If lack of drive isn't a sign of burnout, the struggle stems from a lull in passion. That happens. We all occasionally face the doldrums. Even after purging from ourselves any shining, entangling distractions that lure us from focusing on our call, after resting and refreshing our strength, getting the wheels rolling along again at full speed can be slow.

We may have to give ourselves permission to simply keep at it despite the lack of energizing feeling. Don't be put off. Know that if this is your call, hunkering down with determination to remain faithful often precedes a season of significant growth and fruit. It's not a magic formula. There's really a science to it.

In his book *Think and Grow Rich*, Napoleon Hill put it this way.

"The starting point of all achievement is DESIRE. Keep this constantly in mind. Weak desires bring weak results, just as a small amount of fire makes a small amount of heat. If you find yourself lacking in persistence, this weakness may be remedied by building a stronger fire under your desires."

Hill goes on to say that persistence can become a habit, as evidenced by his years of interviews and analysis of Andrew Carnegie, Henry Ford, Thomas Edison, and 500 other successful people. Because Hill was actually tapping into a spiritual principle, what he thought he discovered 100 years ago still applies today.

Perhaps that's why scriptures instruct us to fan the flame of the Holy Spirit's gift residing in us. The Bible says in 2 Timothy 1:5-7:

---

[17] Thanks Carey, for including me on your book launch team. I appreciated your sharing deeply from your own story to offer challenging insights!

"I am reminded of your sincere faith, which first lived in your grandmother Lois and in your mother Eunice and, I am persuaded, now lives in you also. For this reason I remind you to fan into flame the gift of God, which is in you through the laying on of my hands. For the Spirit God gave us does not make us timid, but gives us power, love and self-discipline."

Have you ever seen someone start a fire from a single spark? It's amazing. A spark is struck into a pile of carefully prepared tinder. It is protectively cupped in the hands. Gentle breath makes it glow brighter until a narrow thread of flame begins dancing in the tinder. More breath. Tiny bits of fuel are added with care not to smother the fragile flame. Incrementally larger fuel is added, from pine needles to twigs, to small sticks. Eventually the fire can consume large logs. But even this strong fire must be tended or it will burn itself out and cool. New fuel must be added, and coals stoked. The borders of the fire must be cared for or damage could result. All from one tiny spark.

Do you see the significant implications?

Look at the progression. Sincere faith, fanned into flame, yields results. Obeying this "fan the flame" command initiates a spiritual transformation from timidity to confidence, from weakness to power. The drive—persistence—is tempered by love. Self-discipline increases. Management of tiny day-by-day decisions bring about significant ministry fruit.

Paul handed this secret for effective service to Timothy. It also applies to you. If you want results on an eternal scale, here's a simple key: Every day fan the flame.

PAUSE & CONSIDER_____

❑ When I ask the question of whether it's
    my time to stop, what brings clarity to
    help confirm my answer?

3.4 THAR SHE BLOWS!

Sometimes it's easy to identify seasoned worship-arts people with a timely call to serve. Like the billowing sea-foam jetting from a whale's spout at sea, you can spot them a mile away.

The telltale signs stand out. You'll notice a servant's heart willing to take on even the least appreciated tasks with an, "I'll get this done right away" attitude. Instead of drawing attention toward themselves, they build up others. They handle well the disappointments inherent to ministry. They show up prepared time after time, and consider the impact on ministry when planning time away.

They're long-timers. They pace themselves so that they can handle the other important responsibilities on their plate and avoid burning out. Not only do they steer clear of entangling sin, they eliminate distractions in their lives that conflict with opportunities to serve. They invest in themselves to continually learn, practice, and improve their ability to serve well. They walk with Jesus steadily, and understand how serving fits into that growth.

That's what I call a challenging laundry list!

The musicians serving in Moses' tabernacle exhibited these traits. Most of their years of service were spent on activities other than playing in the tabernacle. I wonder how many of us would be willing to face such job requirements. Think of yourself spending the best years of your life assigned to temple guard duty, carrying heavy tent poles, polishing utensils, cleaning up after the animal sacrifices, plus fending for your family, all for a slim chance at playing in the tabernacle if—and only if—the miraculous day came in which you beat incredible odds to win the draw and get assigned to perform in the tabernacle at a moment's notice!

Imagine what would have happened had I required the musicians and technicians serving on my church teams to change diapers in the nursery every Sunday they were not assigned to the platform. Would they be willing to trade their in-ears for nose plugs? Out of 110 workers, how many would I have kept? And, just for good measure, what if I additionally required that each volunteer must be prepared to step in and perform at a moment's notice on any given week regardless of the content, key, style, or the likelihood that they almost certainly would not be called upon? Would I have had enough volunteers left to field even a single team?

> *Perhaps part of the difficulty we experience evaluating others is a tendency to evaluate them on performance, and ourselves merely upon intention.*

On one hand, I hungrily picture what could be accomplished with a team of such sold-out, committed members. Then I remind myself that in such a team, I may be the weakest link.

Many worship-arts workers would be too intimidated to serve on such a team, even those who were called to it. Life is more complicated. Even so, I'm finding that sometimes only time can reveal whether a person should continue in their call. Otherwise it's often difficult to tell. Here's an example.

I was asked to become the worship pastor for a congregation in which most of their remaining worship volunteers had experienced significant difficulty. They had been through the wringer. Those who remained were really committed. But one musician specifically caught my attention and I suspected that she was someone who served out of a sense of obligation rather than of call. She seemed to bristle inwardly whenever I tweaked an arrangement, changed a key, or asked the team to step up in any new way. I didn't think she'd last long. I wondered if the time had come for her to stop.

I was so wrong!

She stuck it out. She adapted. She taught herself to move beyond reading notes on a page to be able to create her own parts. She adjusted to in-ears and a click. She made the jump from set teams to role rotations. She practiced. She came prepared to rehearsals. She learned when to not play and how to avoid playing over other people. She sought out training aids and video examples. In addition to her instrument, she worked on her voice and started singing harmony. She even began memorizing music in multiple keys.

At each transition I wondered if this was going to be the last straw. But although her personality was fiercely independent, she became a team player and a huge asset. I really came to respect her tenacious work ethic and her die-hard attitude.

While the team quadrupled to over a hundred musicians and technicians during my time there, she was one of the few originals to outlast me.

She knew her call.

The big question—again

If you want the strength that comes from knowing your call, doesn't it make sense that you have to declare it? Stand on it? Cling to it? List it among the top priorities in your life? Invest in it? Prepare for it, even if the opportunity to serve may be years down the road? Commit yourself to it?

That's why it's healthy to ask the question whether you should stop. It's not that we're looking to stop. Instead, sometimes we need to remind ourselves that now is the time to keep on going. We need to *know* that we know.

My first High School Spanish teacher required commitment. To any student responding half-heartedly or with a hint of hesitation, Mrs. Arbuckle immediately squared off and demanded, "Are you asking me or telling me?" She wanted us to be confident in our answers. She wasn't merely teaching language; she forced us to become brave.

How much more should we embrace our call, our ministry?

So here's the big question that every person must face who is called to serve in worship-arts ministry. It's my question for you. I've asked it before, but you may discover the value of asking often.

Picture yourself being bold in your ministry role. Truly brave. Fix in your mind that image of your amazing potential.

Compare that fantastic image with how you see yourself currently. There are some gaps. (There always are.) What in your life distracts you or stands in your way?

What is one thing—just one thing—that you can do this week to be bold in your commitment to your call?

What can you pray about and say, "Lord, I need you to help me in this area so that I can step up, and without your help, I will dramatically and unquestionably fail?"

So are you called to keep on? Are you asking me or telling me? Know it. Declare it. Stand on it. Be bold!

PAUSE & CONSIDER_____

❏ What stands out to me in this chapter
    and why?

TEAM INFLUENCE

4.0 CONTAGIOUS

Traveling by air is an incredible innovation. Think about it. You pack yourself in a little silver tube, wait a few hours, open the doors, and discover yourself in a new climate thousands of miles away. Incredible!

I realize it's not all fun and games. There's packing the luggage. Traffic. Navigating airports. Parking. Lines to check bags. Lines for TSA. Waiting for the flight. Possible delays or layovers. Landing. Takeoff. Getting luggage. Navigating airport traffic.

Then there's the people. They're crammed into the same silver tube. You share *everything*. You endure the same sounds. You breath the same air. And when someone nearby is continually sniffing, coughing, and sneezing, well, it just makes my skin crawl. It seems like such an easy way to catch something from someone.

People's attitudes make a difference, too. I'm noticing when flying between Chicago/Milwaukee and Sarasota/Orlando that it doesn't take long to begin identifying the contrast between people heading *to* vacation and returning *from* vacation.

If you've traveled, I'm sure you've noticed the excited banter and overall energy of people on the way to experience all their dreams come true. And then on the way home you notice the tired eyes of sunburned parents herding cranky children, all retreating back to their daily routine. Those return trips can seem so much longer!

Isn't it better when traveling with people who are relaxed, comfortable, and excited about reaching their destination? For them, the best is yet to come. I love that sense of anticipation and adventure. It's the one thing on a flight that I don't mind catching.

You've probably seen for yourself that this principle is also true in worship-arts ministry.

We can be infectious. Attitude, behavior, response, presuppositions, language, cultural expression, thoughts, reactions— these are as contagious as the things you encounter onboard an aircraft. And in ministry, when a person invests time and communicates a sense of significance, appreciation, and value for those they address, the more contagious that person becomes.

Whether on a flight, in line at the grocery store, or buying a license at the Department of Motor Services, we've probably all experienced the negative impact when someone forcefully tries to get their own way at the expense of everyone else. Like vinegar in milk, everything turns sour.

These frustrations are very real in worship-arts ministry. Crying children ignored by their parents... bored or angry-looking musicians... people who don't like that you accidentally sat in *their* seat... grammatical errors by the person speaking... team members obviously frustrated because the song element they worked so hard on all week was cut to make way for something they consider far less important... congregants playing on smart phones during the service. I'm sure you can add to the list.

We have plenty of opportunities to draw from the "dark side." As influencers, we have to take responsibility for our impact upon others, too. I know I can become a culprit if I'm not carefully guarding my own heart and attitude.

I'd much rather be the cure than the disease.

If you and I were sharing a row in an aircraft, sitting beside one another in those narrow seats, wouldn't you rather disembark with more love, more joy, more peace? How about more confidence? Or more of a sense that Jesus walks beside you?

I think Jesus likes us to be that kind of contagious.

The Body of Christ is a pipeline for Jesus' touch, provision, and personal connection. Our role in ministry merely serves as a cart Jesus uses to transport His goods.

Serving in worship provides us great opportunity to be Jesus' hands and feet to others. Cultivating influence and how we do ministry helps us carry and deliver more goods. Making good music is the tiny tip of the iceberg.

PAUSE & CONSIDER_____

❑ What are the easiest positive and negative impacts I can have on my teammates or the congregation?

4.1 DELIVERY TRUCKS OF LOVE

We cannot impact the world in a vacuum. It doesn't matter whether you're an introvert or an extrovert, those around you will influence your life for better or for worse. Likewise, you touch others.

When we forget that by withholding ourselves relationally, some people who are desperate for Jesus' touch may not receive what they need. None of us are truly independent.

First, our omnipresent God is always with us. His presence is the medium in which we exist. The molecules of our bones, organs, and muscles fill space already taken up by Him—He *is* the space. All that exists does so in Him. There are no gaps that He does not fill, perhaps other than Hell, the singular location in all that is from which God might have removed Himself. Our every experience, realization, emotion... everything truly, literally occurs in Him.

Additionally, even when we think there's no other person around, we remain in the presence of people. We're actually in pretty impressive company.

The Bible reminds us in Hebrews 12:1:

"Therefore, since we are surrounded by such a great cloud of witnesses, let us throw off everything that hinders and the sin that so easily entangles. And let us run with perseverance the race marked out for us..."

The "cloud of witnesses" being referred to in this passage includes Israel's prophets, kings, judges, martyrs... all those who have gone before us. Imaging a sporting event in which the athlete is allowed to be surrounded by a ring of elite supporters every step of the way. Our reality is kind of like that. We're never truly alone.

And to those of us who are alive, walking now in the flesh on this earth, God Himself additionally promises to be present in a special way when we gather as a group to give ourselves to Him.

The Bible says in Matthew 18:20:

"For where two or three gather in my name, there am I with them."

I wondered about this verse for a long time. It seemed anti-climactic. What's the big deal? God is already *always* everywhere. All creation exists within His presence, like fish exist in the ocean. So why is this verse so important?

I'm discovering that it's actually a really big deal. When Christians come together, God adds extra value. Even though He's always with us, a bonus occurs when "Me and God" becomes "We and God." In this verse the Bible promises that under these circumstances the Lord adds something extra special.

God not only meets our needs personally, but He additionally meets our needs and represents Himself to us by incorporating the gifts He has placed in others. In that way we actually facilitate the interaction between the Church and the Lord.

God designed Relationship to be the primary delivery system through which His loving touch nurtures, feeds, and equips the Church body.

While those around us can cause distraction from our engaging in worship, they may also lend us focus.

Here's a tiny example. In my first role leading a team and congregation, I often found my attention divided by all the details for which I felt responsible. I'm sure you can understand. The transitions, chords, timing, what I wanted to say, the direction and flow of the set, cues for the band and technicians, leading the congregation, watching the clock, the mix, evaluating the congregation's responsiveness, and so on. I could easily lose my sense of worshiping Jesus.

But when I caught myself slipping away, all I had to do was glance at my pianist, Ken. He would be usually lost in worship, focusing on the Lord with an intimate intensity that I admired. Ken served to remind me to keep the main thing the main thing. He furthered me.

The added value that the Lord brings when we gather as a Body comes through us. It comes through you.

Besides, in whatever we face in ministry, when we willingly explore what the Lord may be doing, even relational conflict becomes an opportunity to love and honor Him. Maintaining a humble attitude may enable us to receive Jesus' touch, love, equipping, or grace through others.

We each need the stuff that God designed relationships to deliver.

PAUSE & CONSIDER_____

❑   How does your awareness of everyone
     else in the room impact your role as an
     influential leader during worship?

4.2 MUST BE PRESENT TO WIN

When my sister lost her husband to cancer, she received a flood of cards and letters from all over the world. Potted plants and flowers overflowed the office display counter, the dining room table, the grand piano top, the living room love seat, and the kitchen counter. Friends and extended family provided meals. People stopped in to express care and sympathy.

But what seemed to matter most were those quiet moments when someone would simply be there with her. Powerfully deep emotions and thoughts were conveyed through posture, eye contact, tone, body language. Words failed, but human presence created holy moments.

This holds true in the realm of worship-arts ministry.

A person's presence—their countenance—carries far greater influence than getting the sonic tone exactly right, expressing the song perfectly, or any other part of their performance.

> *Worship at its core remains a spiritual encounter between the Lord and His people. As important as the art is, it remains secondary.*

Musical nuance and excellence remain an important part of providing an effective invitation. But what we're really after is that people accept the invitation and move on to engage with the Lord. Significant things can happen when the people of God gather together in His name according to His purpose.

Obviously, the relational connection of the people in the room has something to do with that "gather together" part. It overrides things like the perfect pedal board signal flow or electronic versus acoustic drum kit debates.

Consider intimate connection to be a "you must be present to win" kind of thing. For me, it helps to fall in love with those I serve.

Keeping yourself separated from the crowd insulates you from God's "gathering together" blessing. You lose the purpose of congregational worship.

We face a tricky challenge. Making that congregational connection competes with dealing with gear, monitor and in-ears concerns, the physicality of the platform and seats, projection, crowd constraints, lighting, and our own awareness. We juggle timing, playing, listening, responsibilities, and all the things that flitter through our minds like, "I wonder what's for lunch."

You know the specific distractions you face.

You can sense it when others face distraction, too.

When you're in the seats, you probably recognize fairly quickly when someone up front begins to disengage. Have you ever watched a person in a church worship team who looks like they'd rather be in bed—or in the dentist chair—or anywhere else rather than on the platform? That really makes you want to connect, doesn't it.

The sad thing is that so many of us behave like we think we're so incredibly good at our craft that people miss noticing we've checked out. But here's the truth: we can't get away with it. It shows.

It signals a slip from worshiping into performance mode.

Ignoring the crowd while staring at a chord chart communicates inability, fear, or a lack of preparation.

In the movie *Back To The Future* it's easy to laugh when the ludicrous character of George McFly ineptly tries to woo the girl by reading a note of someone else's words. And although he is desperately determined to connect with her, his eyes are glued to the note in his trembling, flailing hand.

The distractions get in the way of connection.

How many times have you seen that on a Sunday?

Platform walls, elevated music stands, sealed drum booths, podiums, and even empty physical space all create barriers between the gathered people and those trying to facilitate the gathering. Engaging with the crowd is challenging enough, why add additional roadblocks both in the minds of the congregation and in our own?

One temptation to address this is to overcompensate with extreme gestures and expressions. Being bigger and louder.

Being present doesn't require cheerleaders. It simply means that our actions, body language, our attention, and—lastly—our words convey a single uniform message. "I see you out there, I'm glad to be here with you, we care about each other, and let's get the 'together' part of this worship thing going—isn't the Lord worth celebrating?"

Then go there, together.

PAUSE & CONSIDER

❑ What can I do in my ministry role to influence worship when my mouth is shut, my instrument is silent, and I have no buttons to press?

4.3 CULTIVATING TEAM INFLUENCE

Even if you are not the team leader, you directly impact your teammates. You change the atmosphere and culture in your team. Your attitude is contagious. So are the expectations that you verbally or silently communicate. And although your expectations of others may seem perfectly reasonable to you, they may be premature.

Have you ever found it difficult to serve with someone seeming to think they had the right to ask more from you than they should? Those around you may feel that you may be doing the same thing.

Influence takes time to grow.

When I started leading my first team, I was clueless.

The church where I volunteered as a musician offered me a title and a group of people who agreed to my request that they willingly practice on their own and attend a midweek rehearsal as we prepared for each coming Sunday service.

I had already spent several years as a professional musician. I was comfortable playing music on the platform. I was comfortable with interacting with the crowd. I was comfortable developing songs with professional musicians.

But overseeing a group of volunteers regarding something as personal and diverse as worship?

My approach was simple. I thought of myself as a benevolent director (i.e. dictator) setting a course and pulling everything together.

That approach didn't take me far.

The team graciously complied to my ideas. We were successful. Still, I found myself continually wanting more from them. No matter how hard they tried, I think that they could become discouraged when they sometimes sensed my unspoken dissatisfaction. This cycle occurred completely nonverbally, without a word being said on their part or mine. It was beginning to become wearing.

Thankfully, one day my overseer took me aside. He had recently read a book that, although not directly about worship, had been helpful for him in cultivating influence. Would I be curious enough to take a look?

I was.

He handed me John Maxwell's *Developing The Leader Within You.*[18]

I took the book home and began reading. I remember turning the page about half way through the first chapter and seeing a triangle diagram captioned "The Five Levels Of Leadership."

That content exploded my leadership paradigm. That epiphany repackaged my entire approach to working with others. I always felt that worship volunteers were free to dig deep and give more—I served that way myself—but I had been unconsciously demanding it. I realized that my expectations of my team's level of sacrifice far exceeded what I had earned the right to request simply because I held the Worship Leader title.

Please understand that things had not gotten out of hand. There were no meltdowns. We didn't need emergency meetings. We felt

---

[18] You can imagine my excitement when John released *Developing The Leader Within You 2.0* updated with insights gleaned over the last 20 years!

good about our success. But although I had not voiced my expectations, the pressure on my team was there. Without realizing it, I started pushing people towards burn out. Remaining unchecked, things would have eventually disintegrated. I'd have lost volunteers, and perhaps broken them. They would have paid a deep price for my misunderstanding of ministry and influence. Probably the more passionate they were to serve, the deeper that price could have been.

I realized that I needed to recalibrate my approach. And that's exactly what I did. That was one of those shining moments when I did the right thing in ministry. I am grateful.

This experience is not limited to organizers and team leaders. We each place expectations upon our teammates. Some of those expectations may be in the form of team rules or behaviors we consider to be polite and reasonable. We assume other people are willing and able to invest time and energy at a level similar to ours.

Even without saying a word, when our DEMAND that others comply to our own measure of acceptable service EXCEEDS the influence that we have earned with those people, everyone feels the tension.

Effective influence isn't automatic, particularly when dealing with ministry. It builds slowly through four steps.

1. It starts with a very minimal willingness to treat one another with basic respect.

2. Getting to know one another relationally slowly increases our tolerance for each other's foibles and reveals our shared values. We give each other more of a chance.

3. Experiencing team success adds to that relational grace. By accomplishing our goals together, we appreciate and more willingly receive from one another.

4. As we learn to make each other better, the camaraderie and interdependence expands. We become more positively contagious to others, including those outside the team.

It's a dynamic cycle when deliberately cultivated. Each of these steps to increase your influence with your teammates is impacted by your shared successes and failures. Each step requires maintenance. You can't skip or ignore steps. But each step builds upon the other steps as it grows.

Transform the sense of dissatisfaction and frustration with one another into a sense of iron sharpening iron. That's good influence.

PAUSE & CONSIDER_____

❑ What do I see when I picture the
     impact of this relationship cycle upon
     my team and the congregation? How
     would that impact affect me?

If you do serve in the role of a team leader, music director, worship pastor, or sectional coach, you'll experience far greater long term success, too. Lead the team at a realistic pace. The level of commitment and sacrifice you can expect from others will grow. You'll keep your current musicians and technicians, and attract new ones. Morale will increase. Earning additional influence will expand their willingness to invest more deeply in your vision.

I know that this approach works. In the last church I served, we grew from approximately 25 to 110 musicians and technicians.

Although initial leadership is given to a leader, influence primarily builds over time through relationship, shared experiences, struggles, and harvest. A team willing to follow its leader encourages the leader to grow and delve into new territory, which in turn helps the leader to enable the team to harvest fruit and see their gifts successfully impact worship. It develops into a winning cycle.

Before imparting vision and expectations either as a leader or a team member, consider first investing yourself into your teammates to build relational trust and grace. Your team must know that you care. Realize that every time someone sacrifices to support your values and expectations, you're withdrawing a portion from the deposit of relational grace you have accumulated with that person. Continually replenish that deposit. *Continually.* Celebrate your successes together, whether by officially debriefing as a team, or in unofficial conversations at the water fountain and while dealing with gear at practice.

You'll all succeed.

You will be contagious Jesus-style.

❑   If I came up with two numbers on a scale from one to 10, the first being my level of relational grace with each member, and the second being my level of expectation of them, what can I learn from the difference?

4.4 CONSIDER TEAM RELATIONAL DYNAMICS

Have you ever watched a band disintegrate relationally?

I'm talking about the process of total collapse. Something dark takes root, grows, and festers. It chokes out relational connection. Eventually everything is devoured except bitterness. Dreams have been destroyed, and angry fingers point at one in frustration.

We're saddened to see this happen in secular society, but appalled and surprised when it happens within in church ministry.

It happens anyway.

I guess it's not too surprising. So many of us seem to be relational idiots. Everyone has what's called an *Emotional IQ*. It's your ability to understand your own emotions and to empathize with the emotions of others. All kinds of factors affect it: your upbringing, values, personality, attention, focus... But it's really important because your ability to influence others, particularly in ministry, will be facilitated or hindered by your ability to relationally connect with your team.

And because you are an influencer, remaining relationally open directly affects how your team coalesces.

I dislike other people messing with my ugliness. Most people feel the same way. It's no wonder. Expressing our hearts leaves us vulnerable. Criticism feels painfully personal. Part of transformation means having fleshly, unpleasant things rise to the surface in our lives so they can be addressed. Personally, I'd rather not admit even to myself that such ugliness exist within me, let alone allow others in on what I think is a secret.

Flesh is ungodly, and I don't like revealing that I'm still under holiness construction.

I truly want to experience the greatest me that the Lord designed. I want to honor Him by allowing His pruning and purging, including in my role amongst the rest of His Bride. I want to protect and grow the influence I have. So something in me has to go.

Church relationships can be tricky in any situation. Several key issues regularly arise as culprits specifically in music ministry.

Team Killer #1: A critical spirit

Call it pride, judgment, or self-righteousness—scripture offers many examples of the effect of a critical spirit. It never ends well.

Here's a short list... Goliath mocked God and His soldier David as insignificant; Goliath was killed. King David's wife Michal despised how he worshiped the Lord; Michal was barren for life. Nehemiah's enemies mocked, plotted, threatened, and otherwise attempted to bully him while rebuilding Jerusalem's protective walls; they were thwarted. Haman plotted to defame and publicly execute Esther's cousin Mordecai, because of Haman's bruised pride; Haman was executed. Jesus rebuked his disciples for arguing amongst themselves who was greatest. The apostle Paul corrected his readers many times for treating one another as inferior, whether based upon who performed their baptism, their spiritual gifts, their role, their social status, their ethnicity... You'll find many more examples.

Something in our human nature needs to feel special. We should feel that way; God created us to know our special place in His heart; we're His masterpiece. But instead of finding one's significance in God and in a right relationship with the Body, we can be tempted to generate a sense of significance by finding flaws in those around us.

This issue isn't limited to humanity. Our enemy, Satan fell by it. His proud heart led him to desire the honor that was due only to God Himself. This led to open rebellion and his subsequent fall from authority and position. Now he seeks to defile everything else.

Because sometimes our role in worship-arts ministry is to focus the congregation's worship towards the Lord, it may be easy to begin taking credit for part of that worship. We may listen as our enemy whispers that we are due some of that applause because of our hard work, our skill, our sacrifice... Perhaps finding flaws in our co-servants elevates something within ourselves.

It seems darkly comforting to allow our personal preference to overshadow Jesus' love. Somehow it's easy to assume that what I like, what has worked for me, and what I find easy or comfortable is innately more pleasing to God. But not only is that lie at the heart of much sin, it also keeps dangerous company with the defiler.

Two of the seven abominations to the Lord—things He *really* hates—listed in Proverbs 6:16-19 directly relate to having a critical spirit: haughty eyes and sowing discord among the brethren. Acting on that by exaggerating, falsely accusing, or harming one another—even verbally or by gossip—commits another 3 abominations. So the impact of one's pride upon others should capture our attention.

A critical spirit indicates that our values need tuning. It reveals that my priorities are more focused on myself than on extending Jesus' love. That's a nice way of saying that I'm worshiping me.

A person's value doesn't emanate from skill—the Lord can use any rock, stone, stick, worm, fish, or ass to accomplish His task—that's His choice alone.

We honor the Lord by how we receive one another. Isn't it better to align ourselves with the Holy Spirit's work in each of us? By allowing everyone to shine, we value what the Lord instills in each of us through our growth, gifts, holy passions, and walk with Him. Teams flourish in such an atmosphere!

136

Let's set up each other to succeed. Rather than taking offense for yourself or on behalf of others, consider that the Holy Spirit is already working in them, and that our scope of understanding is smaller than the Lord's. Guarding the flock under our authority should be done restoratively. That's how Jesus wants to work with us, too. Let's follow His example of how to treat one another.

Of all the scriptural passages describing relationships within Church ministry, Romans 12 is one of my favorites. It assesses our treatment of others. Compare this list with what your behavior and words say about your attitude. See how you're doing.

❑ Generous grace for one another

❑ Honoring one another with devotion and sincere love

❑ Hallmarked by patience, generosity, and joy-filled hopefulness

❑ Giving blessing instead of persecution or revenge

❑ Accepting, affectionate, and harmonious unity

❑ Rejoice with rejoicers and mourn with mourners

❑ Faithfully praying

❑ Responding proactively with good, regardless

PAUSE & CONSIDER_____

❑ On a scale of 1-10, how positively
    would I rate my relational impact upon
    my ministry partners?

4.5 TEAM KILLER #2: TAKING ON OFFENSE

Failure to forgive sets a spiritual law in motion that will insulate a person from their own growth, harm others, and desensitize their ability to clearly discern the Holy Spirit's voice in their life. It causes spiritual blinders and hardens hearts. Think of it like building up cholesterol in the blood vessels. It's a killer.

And it's all too easy to find in worship-arts ministry.

The Bible declares in Leviticus 19:18:

"You shall not take vengeance or bear a grudge against the sons of your own people, but you shall love your neighbor as yourself: I am the Lord."

I like how God puts His foot down at the end of that verse. It's like He's saying, "I know you want to take things into your own hands, but I am God, and I say so. End of discussion." [mic drop]

When offended, we're supposed to forgive and bear with one another in love. The Bible is filled with such exhortations. Likewise, when we offend others, it's our responsibility to take the initiative to address the issue.

This mattered to Jesus, and He connected unforgiveness, offense, and responsibility when He said in Matthew 5:23-24:

"So if you are offering your gift at the altar and there remember that your brother has something against you, leave your gift there before the altar and go. First be reconciled to your brother, and then come and offer your gift."

According to Jesus, addressing forgiveness within the Family outweighs the sacrifice of worship.

He didn't say that the offering was negated. He simply said that we cannot allow relationships within the church to hold unaddressed sin if we want worship to occur.

We are responsible to forgive others. We're also responsible to ask for forgiveness. Asking for forgiveness provides a door-opening permission for the other person to extend forgiveness.

It paves the way to transform potential enemies into worship partners.

PAUSE & CONSIDER_____

❑ What will the impact be upon myself if
    I let someone off the hook for an
    offense they caused me?

Team Killer #3: Besetting sin

Besetting sins prevent you from meeting your goals, like mud that cakes and clings on a runners shoes. Sometimes they're called "pet" sins. The list includes porn, overeating, deceit, gossiping, gambling, procrastination, substance misuse, theft... just about anything that feeds your appetites and draws you back for more. Because they appeal to our natural desires, they're a common part of the human experience, mine and yours. Even Jesus was tempted to feed Himself inappropriately. Our culture tends to either excuse the lack of control with a nothing more than a wink as long as no one seems to get hurt.

Even though we all know that such sin can grow dangerously, many of us find ourselves entangled.

This struck home to me forcefully when one of my team members was jailed for an issue that started small and eventually tore his family apart. They've never recovered. He hid it well, that is until the day its ugliness was suddenly publicly exposed. He was convinced that he could take it down on his own. Tragically, he fell into the common trap of thinking that the "your sin will find you out" rule just didn't apply.

It's amazing how creative we humans can be when motivated. We're expert excuse makers.

You know the drill:

- "I didn't mean to..."
- "It won't happen again."
- "I can control it..."
- "It's not that bad..."
- "It helps me deal with _____..."

Honestly, besetting sins have a payoff that feels good, at least for a moment.

That's because a besetting sin often is nothing more than a wrong attempt or short cut to meet a real or perceived need. Once a person believes that their coping mechanism numbs or addresses that need even a little, the hooks take hold. The fear of consequences fades—that is, until the consequences come crashing down.

A besetting sin creates a conflict of interest between our desires and what we know God wants for us. It shouts to us that we lack integrity and gnaws away at our determination and conviction. It builds walls that insulate us from receiving the Lord's protection, insight, and strength.

It specifically destroys ministry relationships in three ways.

1. Besetting sins destroy trust. When issues escalate and consequences become public, like in cases of adultery or sexual abuse, team members feel betrayed. Even the good fruit a person has produced becomes suspect and defiled. People may wonder what other issues lurk in the shadows. Mistrust, suspicion, and fear destroy team building.

2. Besetting sins destroy authenticity. Hiding parts of oneself forces a perpetual false narrative. Honesty falters.

3. Besetting sins remove spiritual discernment. It's like driving a vehicle with mist-covered windows. You cannot distinguish what's ahead. You're not even aware of the countless possibilities you're missing: opportunities for impact, blessings from the Lord, beautiful moments. Even if you may know the road and get by for a while, you cannot see the truck racing toward you.

Pride is a besetting sin's best friend. It whispers that the sin must remain hidden, and feeds the fear of the consequences of discovery. It argues that surely you can handle it on your own. It lies, declaring that things aren't that bad, denying the spiritual ramifications. By listening you become all the weaker because the assets necessary to overcome the besetting sin remain just out of reach. Victory stalls.

Hiding a struggle with besetting sin even from a spouse, accountability partner, counselor, or pastor damages one's walk with God, effective ministry, and one's team. However, *if appropriate*, a team may provide encouragement, prayer support, accountability, and the opportunity to celebrate the success of God's transformational work. It acknowledges that we all face struggles, and embraces the concept that we're better together. It gives permission for everyone to grow. Why withhold that?

PAUSE & CONSIDER_____

❑ What could be the impact of willingly sharing with the rest of my ministry team my besetting sin temptation?

4.6 TEAM KILLER #4: THE DEADLY THREAT OF COMPARISON

Your sweet spot isn't someone else's. Even so, artists, whether musicians or technicians, tend to compare themselves with one another. We pay a lot of attention to how well other people can perform the part that we like to dub "mine."

We notice another's skills, approach, look, talent, fruit, scope, and the responses they garnish from others. This can result in camaraderie and appreciation for what each person brings, but whether from our own insecurity or just plain old curiosity, it can also generate a sense of competitiveness or jealousy.

We're like moths drawn to a flame.

Sometimes we imitate those who we suspect may have an edge on us, thinking that if we can do what they do, we'll experience their fruit. We may fear that if we can't show that we're equally impressive, our offering may be deemed inadequate or irrelevant.

While learning technique from each other is valuable, being led by jealousy, envy, or fear produces bad results. It breeds and feeds something dark inside.

I find it interesting—and more than a little sobering—that the Bible lists Jubal, descendent of Cain the brother-slayer, as the father

of musicians. Envious imitation comes from jealousy, insecurit
fear. Biblical examples consistently teach us that counterfeitir
gifts and callings of others always ends poorly in God's Kingdc
leads to destruction, and you could say that it runs deep in our blood.

I caught myself struggling with jealousy today. I noticed on the
website of a nearby church that they are hosting an upcoming concert
by a musician I didn't recognize. As I read his bio, I saw that he was
recording with someone I did recognize. Impressive. And he's written
a series of kid's adventure stories. Wow, I thought, that looks pretty
good. I'd like that. Must be nice...

Boom. There it was. A little green worm of envy. My enemy was
attempting to sneak past my armor by using the desires of my heart as
a Trojan horse.

Had I allowed it to take root, what could have grown? Perhaps
dissatisfaction with my current role of writing about worship and
leadership and helping churches grow. Perhaps a sense of bitterness
because my current role does not allow me as much opportunity to
play or lead worship. But I love the work that the Lord has called me
to do. Sometimes I must fight to protect it—even from myself.

---

*We each have legitimate goals and values
which the enemy would gladly exploit and
defile if offered a foothold.*

In Hebrew culture, expressions through song and art were part of
worship and everyday life. Excellence was expected in the temple,
but comparison was not. Comparison came from the Greek's
approach to theater and art. The Romans and conquered Jews
learned from them to compare and contrast expressions of worship
and judge them as performances instead of receiving them as
sacrifices.[19] It was natural that the followers of Jesus were likewise
influenced. That could be an example of a time when adapting a
cultural trait from the surrounding dominant culture cost the Church
deeply.

---

[19] Thank you, Don Potter! Your "Cain's Blood" helped me address my own jealousies and fears.
Plus, it took guts to actually sing the whole thing!

This is why the Apostle Paul had to teach the Christians in Corinth to lovingly honor the gifts of one another. They had to be reminded that each believer brings a unique combination of gifts, approaches, personalities, backgrounds, resources, and different resulting fruit. Amidst the backdrop of the incredibly diverse tapestry of the Body of Christ created over centuries of every believer who has, is, or will walk this earth, we each add our unique part. Jesus designed the Church to build this way. No one can add our part for us, and we cannot recreate the part of another. We're custom made.

When we in the Church build one another up, bless one another, complement one another's strengths and gifts, the Church thrives. Good fruit happens.

That's true for you, too.

You are custom made. No one else brings what you do. No one else can ever replace you. The same is true with your team. Shine on!

PAUSE & CONSIDER_____

❑   What is a good way for me to respond
     when I find myself tempted to compare
     my skills and accomplishments to
     those of others?

Moving forward

It's easy to flippantly instruct one another to avoid cultivating a critical spirit, taking offense, giving in to besetting temptation, and making damaging comparisons. The problem is that we simply can't *not have* temptation.

These things are in our nature. They're like weeds after the fall from the Garden of Eden. They're constantly present. Give in and they'll tear our teams and ministry apart. They'll tear you apart, too.

So what do we do with them?

1. **Acknowledge their presence.** They thrive when ignored. Both individually and as a team, understand the normalcy of addressing temptation. Talking about them together helps.

2. **Protect your discernment.** Pursue and eliminate anything in your life that desensitizes your ability to hear the Holy Spirit's voice. Repent and turn from sin. Reduce busyness. Spend time listening. You're the steward and gate keeper.

3. **Utilize your defenses.** Jesus uses our spiritual brothers and sisters to speak into our lives and be the avenue through which He meets many of our needs. Wearing God's armor helps you stand. Reading and applying His Word instructs you and sensitizes you to His assistance.

4. **Dig out the roots.** Don't settle for just saying "No" when tempted. Explore with the Lord what in you makes you vulnerable to this specific temptation. That can be a tip off to a much deeper transformation point in your life. You don't need to do this alone.

Take advantage of temptations. It's like turning the enemy's force against him. They serve as lighthouses drawing attention to the dangerous rocks in your life and amongst your team. Transformation comes when you deal with these temptations well. Isn't that growth worth celebrating together?

PAUSE & CONSIDER_____

❑ What stands out to me in this chapter and why?

4.7 HELPING LEADERS GROW

We're all in some form of transformational process, even our leaders. Leaders don't become great overnight. We can help them become successful and celebrate their fruitful ministry. Or we can suck every ounce of energy and joy from their role.

We all serve under someone else's authority. Whether it's a church board, an elder, a pastor, a staff person, a worship leader, a music director, a section leader, an influential congregational member, or the Lord Himself, you serve under a leader.

Whether we talk about the New Testament churches, or the Old Testament tabernacle, temple, or kingdom, or the Heaven on Earth Kingdom, we find biblical examples of having human leaders. The Lord accepts responsibility for their placement, and requires submission from us.

We need leaders. They pull together all the different necessary roles. They carry the torch of vision. They equip and facilitate us as we serve and grow.

However, just like Elijah explained to the Israelites asking for a King to lead them, there is a downside.

Leaders are humans in transition. They're in the middle of a steep learning curve, which can cost us dearly. They make mistakes. Sometimes they're not easy to follow.

But sometimes we're not easy to lead.

❏ What comes to mind when I consider what makes me an easy or difficult person to oversee?

A mile in uncomfortable shoes

Leading is tough.

Leaders face continual change. Every program type and church size requires different skills and approaches. What may have worked in the past may not anymore. New systems need development or old systems need to adapt. And they have to lead *us*.

Leaders handle concerns on a wider scale than our own. We have the luxury of focusing on all the tiny details regarding our role. Those serving over us must fit our piece of the puzzle into the bigger picture, including factors about which we are unaware.

I'm not sure whether the most difficult part of leading is the role itself, the personal sacrifice, or leading difficult people. But I know that when my team has my back, I am strengthened to face the other challenges.

Asset or anchor?

Have you ever heard this? "I'd love being a shepherd, if it weren't for all the sheep."

We sheep can make things tough for a leader. Sometimes we obstinately run our own direction. Occasionally it's what we *don't* do. In a recent online poll I conducted, 65% of worship leaders indicated that their greatest discouragement comes from relying on people who fail to respond to communication.

While we may not be able to choose how our leaders approach their roles, we can choose how we respond to their leadership.

Our attitudes can be hard to keep in check. Our expectations don't always line up with our leader's approach or strength. We may be unaware of significant factors influencing their choices. Sometimes we assume that they make their own decision, when the unpopular instructions may actually be handed down by the person in authority over our leader. We may allow our attitudes to be impacted by the almost inevitable frustration arising while aligning parts of music into a unified whole.

How can you know whether you are an asset or an anchor?

The easiest way is simple. Schedule an appointment for a short discussion or phone call. When you meet, simply ask. Here's a script.

"On a scale of 1-10, how would you say I'm doing in supporting you as a leader?" ...Listen. "Why do you pick that number?" ...Listen. "How can I support you and the team better?" ...Listen.

You may be amazed at what you learn.

PAUSE & CONSIDER_____

❑ Considering that the Lord ultimately places
  people in positions of authority, what do
  my words and behaviors toward my leader
  say about my attitude toward Jesus?

4.8 THE DIRTY 10-LETTER WORD...

Many cultures around the world, including here in the United States, place a high value upon personal independence. That tends to make us difficult people to lead.

Especially concerning personal expression and spirituality, we struggle if serving conflicts with our preferences. If mistrusting authority, we sometimes undermine those who oversee us. We second guess their decisions, preferences, motives, and attitudes, even without realizing the full picture they must consider. We blame them for our own failures, conflicts, and shortcomings. When we're unreliable and difficult to lead, we can push them toward walking away from the Lord's call on their life.

When we are in agreement with our leader and things seem to go smoothly, it's easy to think that we're following well. But when following costs us more than we want to pay, our true colors show. *Submission* begins the moment we disagree with our leader.

The Bible addresses this in Hebrews 13:15-18. The verses form a scriptural sandwich—a bun with meat in the middle. Verse 15 and 16 are the bottom of the bun, reminding us to continually offer sacrificial praise, including in the way we treat others. The top of the bun is verse 18, reminding us to pray and live honorably.

The meat of the sandwich is verse 17. It instructs us to serve with confidence in our leaders. It reminds us that our leaders are accountable to God and commands us to submit to their authority. The reason is simple. We are to make their work be a joy, not a burden. By honoring our leaders, we honor the Father.

This passage also says that failing to submit is self-defeating. Remember the goal that leaders work to attain? Ephesians 4:12-13 says that they equip us to serve so that we can mature and become more like Jesus.

When we become a burden to our leaders,
our transformational growth ceases.

When leaders are out of line

How can we best serve under leaders who seem to make poor choices, commit significant errors, or hit the wall of their own limitations? For us, facing this can be a personal crisis.

If the issue is outright sin, particularly resulting in causing harm, it may be appropriate to follow the Matthew 18:15-17 instructions.

Otherwise, the Bible offers few options.

One sobering example is in Exodus 12. Moses, the leader of Israel and the man whom God considered as friend, was not following his own law forbidding marriage to a non-Hebrew. Moses' brother Aaron (Israel's high priest) and sister Miriam (a prophetess of Israel) confronted him. The result? God struck Miriam with leprosy.

Years ago someone suggested that Aaron and Miriam were using the issue to play for power. I don't see that in the passage myself, but the text does suggests to me that when it comes to supporting our leaders, we may have the details right while still being in the wrong.

God takes submission seriously.

I'm reminded that God places people in leadership. He can just as easily remove them. Nothing takes Him by surprise. He has a plan.

Doesn't that suggest we should consider our steps carefully?

Here's an example of the blessing that can come from reacting slowly. One of the best small group leaders I ever had always claimed he was a terrible leader. He realized that he didn't have any of the skills needed for a small group to be successful. Rather than looking for a different leader, our group rallied behind him. He decided to delegate everything to whichever person seemed best suited to that particular task. He saw to it that nothing fell through the cracks. Our support of him helped him blossom into a fantastic leader, and his leadership enabled us to become a successful, vivacious group.

Sometimes a fault in leadership is actually a catalyst in disguise for you to rise and—with the leader's blessing—fill a need. Grow.

Iron sharpens iron

We have the opportunity to enable our leaders to shine. One of my favorite examples comes from scripture.

Consider the story of Prince Jonathan and his armor bearer. War was going on between their country of Israel and raiding parties from the neighboring Philistines. The Israelites were poorly armed and the conflict seemed to have run to a standstill. So Jonathan and his personal assistant snuck away from King Saul's army to examine the enemy's outposts. Jonathan asked his armor bearer whether he'd follow Jonathan in an attack, adding, "Maybe God will help out." Jonathan's simple plan for the two of them: Announce themselves to the enemy outpost. Scale the cliff face while vulnerably exposed. Take on an entire garrison of 20 or more warriors.

Jonathan's unnamed soldier agreed. As a team, Jonathan drove through the enemy and the armor bearer finished those they passed. The Philistines panicked, King Saul realized something was up and pressed the advantage. Israel scored a great victory.

The armor bearer could have said, "No. Your idea is crazy. Let's stick with the army." That was the smart thing to do. King Saul wouldn't be pleased with an armor bearer agreeing to help his son fool heartedly attack an enemy garrison on his own. Perhaps Jonathan would have continued on despite a negative response, but I doubt it. Even though he trusted in God's intervention, he knew that he needed someone to partner with him and watch his back.

Leaders need trustworthy followers.

I know firsthand the blessing that comes from overseeing a team I could depend upon to support my leadership. We shared a mutual confidence that only arises when a team trusts its leader to not abandon them, and the leader knows that even if jumping off a cliff and falling flat, the team will embrace the plunge. Such willingness grows from having faced difficult battles together and prevailing.

That's a victorious combination.

Being an asset

These 6 steps help me bring out the best in my leader and myself.

1. Pray for the leader's success and that I can be an asset to make their work a joy.

2. Support the leader directly and behind their back.

3. Take initiative to do my job as unto the Lord (without prodding, slipping, complaining, sucking energy, or requiring handholding).

4. Communicate by word and deed that I remain an ally.

5. Ask the leader privately if there is anything I can do to help, and then complete it right away.

6. Privately brainstorm with other team members about blessing the leader with opportunities to breathe, refresh, and seek growth ideas.

PAUSE & CONSIDER_____

❑ How can I become a vital part of my leader's growth?

5

SACRIFICE OF PRAISE

5.0 WHAT GOES ON THE ALTAR

When the ancient Hebrews approached God's altar to worship, they knew not to come to the temple empty handed. Everyone brought something to give. They had many forms of sacrifices, including freewill offerings, sin offerings, thanksgiving offerings, tithes, and a smorgasbord of ways to approach God.

People serving in worship-arts ministry face our own altar of sacrifice. Approaching it well opens the door to transformation and protects us from the ministry failure that results from other approaches. We have vital lessons to learn from the Hebrews.

They needed some rules. Before they formalized proper ways to offer sacrifices, things tended to get messy. The first altar sacrifice by humans in scripture was such a fiasco that it literally ended in murder.

Through Moses, God provided sacrifice rules. They were serious and meticulously spelled out. But almost immediately after Moses anointed Aaron and his sons to be the priests assigned to carry out and oversee all the sacrifices of Israel, the two eldest sons did things their own way. They died on the spot.

But the people of Israel paid attention. They wanted to approach God's altar properly. For example, they gave so generously of the valuables they brought from Egypt that Moses actually asked them to stop. Perhaps that was the only offertory in history to end prematurely! When they did as Moses instructed, God showed up in mighty and tangible ways. We want God to move in our services, too.

Lambs were the primary sacrificial animal. They had to be perfect. The Hebrews understood that the lamb represented the person offering the sacrifice. Second-rate offerings meant second-rate hearts.

Outward represents inward.

This concept was central to Hebrew faith. It's even reflected in their language. Every Hebrew word for praise associates an outward physical action with an inward spiritual interaction with God.

Not only did the sacrifice represent the person's current state, it reflected the intended state of their heart as a promise of what it was to become. Faulty gifts prophetically announced a continuing dishonoring of the Lord. The altar sacrifice represented the past, present, and the future condition of the person giving the offering.

> *What we put on the altar—what you bring to the Lord—matters. Just like the Hebrew's lamb, your music and your acts of service declare the condition of what they represent: your heart.*

PAUSE & CONSIDER

❑ If my "sacrifice of praise" declares what I anticipate my walk with the Lord to become, what have I predicted?

Fattening our lamb

Fast forward about a century from Moses' to Malachi's day. By this time things had fallen apart. People became so apathetic that it wasn't worth the effort to even try collecting tithes. The priests fended for themselves, and eventually temple duties degraded into not much more than an afterthought. The expectations of the people were so low that this state of affairs seemed not to bother them. They felt it was good enough.

What do you think that said about the condition of their hearts?

> *Deliberately offering less than our best—*
> *withholding from the Creator and Master*
> *of the Universe what's legitimately due*
> *Him from each of us—betrays a dangerous*
> *contempt for God.*

God held the priests in Malachi's day accountable for the sloppy and unacceptable sacrifices. Consider the ramifications of being a priest cursed by God!

It makes sense that instead we should want to offer the most excellent gift to our Lord that we can give. Wouldn't you think that such a desire would lead us to diligently hone our talent and become skilled craftsmen? I call that "fattening the lamb."

Something significant happens in us when we operate out of a childlike desire to offer significant, extravagant gifts to our King. Our Heavenly Father delights in His children. I don't think He can help but respond. He blesses us in the resulting interaction by increasing the fruit of His Spirit in us.[20]

In other words: He blesses us with transformation.

PAUSE & CONSIDER_____

❑   How can I balance giving my best, handling
    the other responsibilities in my life, and
    joy?

---

[20] Spiritual Fruit: love, joy, peace, patience, kindness, gentleness, goodness, faithfulness, and self-control (Galatians 5:22-23)

5.1 THE VALUE OF AUTHENTICITY

Quality alone does not always reflect the heart. Consider the scene in *The Music Man* when the boy's marching band finally performs. The parents view the painful note-missing, instrument-squawking performance through a lens of love and pride. To their eyes and ears, it is absolute perfection. You've possibly seen a similar reaction to a children's Bible School production.

When the hearts of the audience engage in worship, God's grace extends. Perhaps that's why Psalms 100:1 instructs us to make a joyful noise unto the Lord. It literally commands us to shout with joy. The Lord invites us to go for it with all we've got and withhold nothing.

A person's value or spiritual significance is unrelated to the level of their artistic ability. Jesus' willingness to shed His blood for you came from His love for you, not because He was impressed by the artful ambience of your patches at last night's gig.

> *Your identity is not found in your expression, but rather in Jesus.*

Likewise, I don't believe that God cares about the quality of what we offer for its own sake. He is far more interested in the "heart motivation" behind what we're offering Him—worshiping in spirit and in truth.

Excellence in our preparation and offering is really God's gift to us. It helps us know we've offered our best. It's how we embrace authenticity. When we fail to give our best, that knowledge sticks with us. We know we settled for less. Authenticity gives way to pretending.

King David is probably one of our greatest examples of being an authentic worshiper. I am continually challenged by his refusal to offer God sacrifices which cost himself nothing. He knew that personal sacrifice contains a greater blessing.

Congregations are hungry. Our authentic worship invites them to permit themselves to follow our example and engage. "Join us, taste and see that the Lord is Good! Come on in, the water's fine!"

Excellence versus authenticity

Most likely every person comes out at a somewhat different point on the Excellence versus Authenticity continuum. We can argue about it all day and never come to complete agreement.

Here's the point. We can do both. We can give our all *and* give it to the best of our ability. Certainly we can strive to improve on both points, but when we can walk away knowing that we put it all out there—skill, preparation, camaraderie, attitude, heart, mind, soul, and interaction with the Lord—our *utmost*, we can walk away satisfied with the lamb we gave.

> *The difficulty is that sometimes the Excellence versus Authenticity debate is really a cover for a deeper issue: Trying to determine how little we can get away with and still call it good enough.*

Everyone comes to their own balance of time and resources to handle everything on their plates. That affects our opportunity to prepare for serving with excellence. Considering that the responsibilities of life seem to continually shift that balancing point, the struggle never goes away.

A personal note on preparation

My commitment to excellence drives my time on the platform or behind the board. It also directly impacts my personal preparations. If I cannot be on-site, on-time, and prepared for every rehearsal and service, I arrange for someone else who can. It means that I make every attempt to communicate proactively with teammates and leadership. I consider how to do my role well to avoid making distracting mistakes that could shift the focus of my leaders, teammates, or congregation from the Lord.

You may have noticed by now that details matter to me. A lot. So it won't surprise you that it takes a while for me to practice and carefully weave my part into the team's overall texture. I don't mind spending that time. Preparation allows the Holy Spirit time to work in my heart for whatever fruit God wants to harvest.

That's a worthwhile exchange.

God treasures praise offered with integrity and purity, and it seems that He often responds proportionately to the level of sacrifice we are willing to offer Him of ourselves.

PAUSE & CONSIDER_____

❑   How can a team balance differing views of
     excellence and authenticity?

5.2 WE'RE THE LAMB

The Bible says in Mark 12:30:

"Love the Lord your God with all your heart and with all your soul and with all your mind and with all your strength."

Our worship expressions all stem from presenting ourselves to the Lord as a *living sacrifice*. This means giving up our rights of ownership over our identity, heart, thoughts, will, body, creativity, relationships, expressions, time, resources, and emotions. We declare Him to be Lord of every element that makes up our lives, with every point of our interaction with reality.

Call it "full-self" worship.

This God-honoring worship engages us in a continual process of laying these parts of ourselves upon His altar. We crawl onto the altar and tenaciously stay there. If you're like me, occasionally you have to remind yourself to climb back on in a particular area of life.

However, a person can attend a worship service—or serve in one—and behave exactly the same as everyone else in the room, and yet fail to worship at all. Worship is not the trappings we associate with music. It's not choir robes, organ music, a somber mood, incense, candles, skinny jeans, beards, cool pedal boards, beating drums, or textured loops.

Even so, it's easy to get caught up in all of that. I have.

Forms of expression which we associate with worship are not innately worship in themselves. They simply depict, enact, or represent the worship of a person's heart. They are cultural, editable, changeable, omitable, and improvable.

Worship involves a choice on the part of the worshiper to give adoration and to ascribe worth to God. This choice may occur in one of many forms, and may involve revelation, reflection, response, praise, prayer, examination, confession, giving, scripture reading, preaching, giving testimony, or expressing affirmations of truth. But ultimately, we're the lamb of our sacrifice.

Know your expressions

Almost every biblical example of worship involves some form of physical expression, including singing, bowing down, shouting, clapping, lifting hands, playing instruments, leaping, dancing, prostrating one's self, being silent, and kneeling. (For some reason, I find it rather ironic that the one posture not mentioned in the Bible as appropriate for worship is sitting.)

Some of these probably express your heart better than others.

An expression's efficacy doesn't make it holy or universal. My avenue may not be yours. What's important is identifying what works for us and our congregations. Whether an old favorite or a new expression, the danger is in relying upon a form itself instead of upon our sacrifice and resulting transformation.

PAUSE & CONSIDER_____

❑   How can I extend permission or model expressions of worship which have little meaning to myself but significant meaning to others?

Meaningful expressions demonstrate themselves when we are free to uninhibitedly respond to what God is doing in our hearts.

The Bible is full of examples of such emotional expression. And while the techniques we use to perform these expressions change culturally, it is fascinating to see that the need for such expression never goes away.

Although music (with or without singing) almost always accompanies biblical examples of worship, it is not absolutely necessary. However, music provides an effective doorway for connecting human hearts to God and to one another as we praise Him. It can bypass our mental filters and connect directly with our soul. God gave music power to give voice to our hearts.

How we wield it matters.

Culturally relevant expressions

Did it ever bother you that the New Testament does not give a lot of instructions for *how* to express praise? It mentions gathering as a group, singing, praying, preaching, and teaching, but it doesn't really say *how*. Yet the Old Testament explained things in such minute detail.

Why the difference?

It turns out that there's a very important reason that directly impacts how we express worship today. Knowing this answer helps protect us from getting stuck by locking in on forms of worship that have grown irrelevant and ineffective.

The Old Testament was written to one single specific culture out of the entire world. They were God's chosen people. Their specific worship expressions helped define their culture and instill identity.

The New Testament extended the call to become God's people into every culture of the world. Consider the Apostle Paul's "be Roman to the Romans and Jewish to the Jews." Expression is cultural.

Culture provides context that gives the expression meaning. The heart part of the sacrifice—the intention being expressed—extends beyond cultural forms.

You no longer need to be Jewish in order to understand expressing worship to God. Your culture counts.

So while the message of the sacrifice is common to all humans, the actual packaging of how worship expresses itself can be full of variety.

Forms of expression are merely the cultural package we use communicate our message to our target audiences of humans, spiritual beings, and the Lord God Himself. We craft the package, be it a hymn or today's newest contemporary release.

It makes sense that we hold significance in the form. Our cultural forms help provide understanding. But forms having truly run their course can be set aside. Our challenge is to avoid disenfranchising someone by discarding their important expressions.

PAUSE & CONSIDER_____

❏   What do I do if my expressions of worship differ greatly from my teammates' or congregation's expressions?

5.3 PACKAGING WELL

I understand that we can't get too hung up on tradition or form of expression, and that such things pale in importance to what the sacrifice actually represents. Still, the package contains a declaration of the heart's condition. Because this matters, it bears continued exploration.

I have to think that perhaps the actual investment we make in crafting our expression helps further impress its meaning into the very DNA of our hearts. Like simmering a soup condenses its flavors, creating the worship package allows meaning to intensify. The package itself becomes valuable not only through its message, but also through what it imparts during the crafting process.

Shouldn't the package reflect the value of what it contains?

Occasionally when I arrive at a church to help strengthen or develop their worship program, they greet me with some kind of "glad you're here" welcome gift, often a snack or a token that's representative of their region. While it's certainly nothing I request or expect, I feel appreciated. But no one has ever offered one of these gifts simply contained in a plastic grocery bag.

It's natural for us to want the appearance of the outside to reflect the intent of the inside. Every culture gives gifts, and in every culture the package has significance.

Our worship expressions reflect something very precious to God, the gift of ourselves. While we could never match the extravagance with which He loves us, it is fitting that we pour ourselves out fully in gratitude to Him. Package it well.

PAUSE & CONSIDER_____

❑ God poured out Himself for us when we did not deserve it. How can I similarly pour myself out this week in a way that exceeds expectations and adds value to my leaders, team, and congregation?

Damage Control

But what if the package—the expression—becomes damaged?

What if you mess up? What if the announcement for the Popsicle Stick Christmas Tree Ornament Fundraiser went long and your special song was cut? What if the sound technician was distracted by someone complaining about the volume, and consequentially missed turning up the volume for your solo? What if the senior pastor decided 2 minutes before the service that he needed 5 extra minutes for his funny illustration and required that the ministry song be cut?

If you've served in worship-arts ministry for very long at all, I'm sure you can think of an example from your own experience.

Did your lamb become ruined? Was the gift created by you and the team squandered?

That's a heart wrenching question with a simple answer: With any sacrifice, once it's offered, it isn't ours anymore.

God accepts it. He gets to use it however He wants, even if that use is different than we intended and no one else gets to share it. A sacrifice with strings attached isn't truly a sacrifice.

You have the graceful knowledge that the Lord knows your heart. He still received your offering.

He knows the hours you poured into preparation. He understands your intentions. He gathers that all up to Himself. He alone has the right to decide how to use that sacrifice. To Him, your offering, given freely and of a pure heart, is acceptable however He decides to use it.

Sometimes the Jews' offerings were completely consumed on the altar. Other times they were able to eat a bit of it or share it with God's priest and temple helpers, and still other times it was a feast.

Our job as worship workers is to package our best offering to accurately reflect the heart of a congregation as we come before the Lord in the grace and cleansing action of Jesus.

> *Clearly, offering a sacrifice packaged in anything but our best is unworthy of either the gift it contains or of the gift's receiver, whether it gets consumed in a puff of smoke, or if we get to enjoy the barbecue.*

Things going "wrong" provides one of the best opportunities for the Lord to test your heart. Your response becomes your next lamb.

Talk about a trying test!

Who benefits the most

There's another factor. I'm thinking that we—the Church—often receive the most blessing out of worshiping. It's really not a fair deal to God.

I've had opportunity to play with much better musicians than I'll ever be, regardless of the hours I invest in practice. Is the Lord getting the short end of the stick when I'm on the platform? Does He say to the saints gathered around the throne, "Oh, too bad, I see Tim's on today" and shrug his shoulders? Surely the angels, unencumbered by humanity's limitations and able to see God face-to-face in His very presence, offer technically superior praise.

The Lord isn't made better by the excellence of our worship. God simply delights in our hearts and blesses us in return. When we come before Him in true worship, He shows up and pours Himself out upon His people. We're blessed and changed by His presence. He doesn't mind getting the short end of the stick—He loves to love us. And His response to our praise seems to me—and perhaps you'll agree—to be proportional to how much of ourselves we invest in the giving.

PAUSE & CONSIDER_____

❑ When what I've prepared as an expression of worship doesn't happen the way I planned, how does my response reflect upon the Lord?

MOVING FORWARD

6.0 YOUR DO/BE BALANCE

For years I worked hard to iron out every moment in my worship sets. I crafted transitions into, out of, and even within each song. I considered the layering of the instrumental voicings, the overall development of the song, how the music/lyric blend built a framework for worship expression possibilities, the special nuances each musician and vocalist personally added, the impact of visuals, and all kinds of other elements.

Maybe I went a little overboard.

Most of us work hard to ensure that each song facilitates a special place in the overall tapestry of our congregational expressions of worship. I'm guessing you may agree that nuances matter.

I can get overly caught up in details.

I remember one particular fail. Before a concert the rest of the band I played with had gathered in the Green Room at the designated time to pray that the Lord would pull on people's hearts through our music. One of the guys wondered why I was missing. He found me backstage straightening cables and copying the finalized set list for the techs. He simply shook his head, muttered, "Martha, Martha," and returned to the group. Apparently I was too busy for prayer.

Ouch!

Even though nitty-gritty details can provide connection points for people like me, I must continually remind myself that worship is not about the details.

You may know someone similar. Perhaps you're one yourself.

I've found that roughly 70% of us in worship-arts ministry struggle with details that distract our focus from the Lord. The rest of us struggle with the people in the first group. Then the first group struggles with the second group's inability either to complete the details or to get them right. Next the second group struggles with the first group's inability to enjoy how the songs connects us with Jesus. This results in the first group accusing the second group of dishonoring Him with slipshod work. Now the gloves are off and everyone is simply struggling with one another.

At some point in this spiraling cycle the team forgets the reason they're there. Joy and passion go out the window.

We, like Mary and Martha, attempt to merely tolerate one another, swallowing our irritation and complaining. Some of us focus on loving Jesus by taking care of the details. Others focus on loving Him by sitting at His feet. In our attempts to keep the important thing the important thing, we lose our sense of balance and settle—at best—for staying out of each other's way.

Unity fails.

While in this state, we invite others to connect?

This collapse happens because we're the people responsible with facilitating the songs and the details of our congregational services. We must give significant attention to the tools and responsibilities we wield or we couldn't accomplish our tasks. But giving too much attention loses our "why." We miss significant things that can happen during congregational worship times as our souls reach out to the Lord, stretching, bowing, breaking, and surrendering.

I'm amazed how easy it is for me to become distracted from the fact that worship is all about Jesus. That's hard to admit, isn't it?

❑ What helps me realize that I might be struggling with losing focus on the Lord while serving?

In this ongoing tug-of-war, I find it helpful to continually remind myself that fruit comes from walking with Jesus. I can't fake that, force it, buy equipment to fix it, or exchange preparation for it. I've even resorted to placing reminders on my charts and pedal boards to help me keep the right focus. Because planning is important for me, I also remind myself that leading is more about following the Lord than following my plan. As I learn to stay out of His way, I connect with Him better personally and point people to Him more effectively.

I've compiled this list of 12 common distractions raised by various church music teams I've assisted. On a scale of 1 (low) to 5 (high), rate the level of distraction each of these commonly becomes for you.

1 — 2 — 3 — 4 — 5 Equipment quality, condition, and playability

1 — 2 — 3 — 4 — 5 Team members having conflicting expectations and commitment levels

1 — 2 — 3 — 4 — 5 Relational connections during rehearsal

1 — 2 — 3 — 4 — 5 The level of complexity in song arrangements

1 — 2 — 3 — 4 — 5 Systems for team communication

1 — 2 — 3 — 4 — 5 Micromanagement or lack of knowledge by church authorities regarding worship-arts ministry issues

1 — 2 — 3 — 4 — 5 Rehearsal regularity or length

1 — 2 — 3 — 4 — 5 Congregational attitude regarding preferred worship styles and expressions

1 — 2 — 3 — 4 — 5 Learning new music, concepts, and skill development

1 — 2 — 3 — 4 — 5 Current team organizational structure and approach

1 — 2 — 3 — 4 — 5 Connecting with the congregation during services

1 — 2 — 3 — 4 — 5 The results your serving seems to produce

These details form the infrastructure of serving. They must be addressed, or imagine the resulting train wreck. But whether we love or hate them, we must learn to address them in a way that frees us to embrace the Lord while He works even more deeply than we can comprehend.

But handling them creates potential conflict and takes precious time. On the one hand, we cannot ignore them. On the other hand, we cannot lose our focus on the Lord. On the other hand, we can't forget the congregation. But we can't forget to follow the leadership. And we can't forget the other responsibilities in our lives. By now we've run out of hands.

PAUSE & CONSIDER_____

❑ Of all the distractions my team faces when serving, how difficult would it be for us to all agree on which distraction is the most significant?

6.1 JESUS' FOCUS

Did you wonder about Jesus' "why" for taking on flesh? The nuances go beyond the simple, "He came to save us." They help us balance *doing* for Jesus and *being* with Him.

John 1 describes Jesus as the Word of God. He is God's declaration encapsulated into action, through which all created things—including us—are made. For me, a former English teacher, it makes sense to think of Jesus as the essential, causational verb of God, the physical embodiment of God's will.

> *Jesus doesn't merely represent God or point the way to God. Jesus IS God fully physically manifested—expressed in sound, light, and flesh. Wherever Jesus is, at that place God is completely, personally present and in action. Jesus IS God Incarnate.*

It's like the difference between the Spanish verbs *ser* and *estar*. Both mean "to be" and translate into some of the most basic words in English like *am, are, is, was, were,* and *will be.* You may remember your English teacher talking about these foundational "be" verbs. They were highlights in your educational journey, I am sure!

In Spanish these two words are distinctly different. *Estar* is more temporary, like whether I *am* feeling hungry or warm at this moment; it's a current state of being that may change. *Ser*, on the other hand, has a sense of permanence of the foundational nature of something, like how I *am* my father's son. Nothing changes that.

Jesus is the *"ser"* of God, expressed in human form. This goes beyond whatever Jesus happened to be doing or teaching on a particular day. Expressing God was even deeper than His DNA. He literally *is* God's living human expression.

Jesus explained why He became human, walked among us, and sacrificed Himself for His Bride. He said He came so we could experience Life to the absolute fullest measure that it could provide, living and walking with the Father in the very way for which we were created. In other words, Jesus' *transformational love* completes His action of creating each of us as the person He envisioned even before the foundation of the world.

Jesus also shared with the disciples that He came to reveal the Father. He wasn't interested in the credit stopping with Himself. When we look at Him, He wants us to see and experience Almighty God directly.

The Bible says in Hebrews 1:3:

"The Son is the radiance of God's glory and the exact representation of His being, sustaining all things by His powerful word. After He had provided purification for sins, He sat down at the right hand of the Majesty in heaven."

I really like how the Bible shares one moment when Jesus explained this to the disciples in John 14:5-13:

"Thomas said to him, 'Lord, we don't know where you are going, so how can we know the way?'

"Jesus answered, 'I am the way and the truth and the life. No one comes to the Father except through me. If you really know me, you will know my Father as well. From now on, you do know him and have seen him.'

"Philip said, 'Lord, show us the Father and that will be enough for us.'

"Jesus answered: 'Don't you know me, Philip, even after I have been among you such a long time? Anyone who has seen me has seen the Father. How can you say, 'Show us the Father'? Don't you believe that I am in the Father, and that the Father is in me? The words I say to you I do not speak on my own authority. Rather, it is the Father, living in me, who is doing his work. Believe me when I say that I am in the Father and the Father is in me; or at least believe on the evidence of the works themselves. Very truly I tell you, whoever believes in me will do the works I have been doing, and they will do even greater things than these, because I am going to the Father. And I will do whatever you ask in my name, so that the Father may be glorified in the Son. You may ask me for anything in my name, and I will do it.'"

You could probably make a case that a good subtitle for the Bible could be *See Jesus, See God*.

Did you notice what Jesus added at the end of this passage? It's vitally important. If we believe in Him, He declares that we can do what He did.

What exactly *did* He do?

He revealed the Father.

But we can't do that very well while spinning out of balance.

Jesus' balance

The Bible connects Jesus' incarnation with the topic of balance in Colossians 1:15-20.

"The Son is the image of the invisible God... in him all things were created: things in heaven and on earth, visible and invisible... all things have been created through him and for him... in him all things hold together. He is the head of the body, the church... so that in everything he might have the supremacy... all God's fullness dwells in him, and through him to reconcile to himself all things...."

Jesus *is* God. Jesus holds together all the details and aligns everything—including you and me—with Himself. Jesus brings all things into proper balance. Even the details. With His help, we can get the balancing part right, too.

> *Those of us who are do-ers must learn to BE with Jesus amidst the doing. Those of us who are be-ers must learn to DO with Jesus amidst the being. This is part of our transformation process, and we need Jesus' help.*

The balance comes when we align with Him in both doing and being. Our goals, approach, and timing need to match His. Then we realize His presence in full, regardless of our approach.

PAUSE & CONSIDER_____

❑ How can I best point people toward Jesus when I'm facing lots of responsibilities that I must address?

6.2 ADDRESSING FEAR OF FAILURE

Jesus' goals include loving us, transforming us, and revealing the Father. Jesus' goals are compatible. They go hand in hand. As we see Father God for who He really is and experience His love, we cannot help but be transformed. It can become a self-perpetuating process.

Fact #1: Jesus has unlimited ability to impact people through us regardless of our level of skill or competency. How liberating!

Fact #2: When we maintain balance, we demolish roadblocks which significantly hinder that impact. How challenging!

There's a balance we must each find between do-ing and be-ing. Get it wrong, and the misbalance can become deadly to effectively serving in worship-arts ministry. Get it wrong, and we'll almost certainly fall into the trap of trying to accomplish through our own strength what only He can do.

Allow me to specify. I'm not talking about sin in our lives that mar His light from shining through us. I'm not talking about how our mistakes can distract people from looking to Him; that's a much smaller issue easily addressed through preparation.

The misbalance comes when we take our eyes off Him just long enough that we no longer notice that our hands have replaced His on the steering wheel. We're talking about allowing necessary tasks to slip by undone because we must choose between either being "spiritual" or being "relational."

We need to be both. If we choose one and omit the other, things spin out of balance.

It's just as ludicrous to say, "Not now, Jesus, I'm rewiring the stage" as it is to say, "Not now, Jesus, I'm praying."

Both sides of the balance equation can get it wrong. Balance doesn't mean *equal time*. How distracting would be ensuring a one-to-one ratio of time spent on being and doing? Trying to accomplish the fruit of Jesus' work when we've lost our focus on Him usually means that we have resorted to operating merely within our own strength.

> *Human effort, regardless of how artistically crafted, passionately presented, or spiritually pious, cannot force Jesus to move. Our power cannot replace His.*

Over time we can learn to tune in to Him amidst both doing and being. It takes practice. We have to catch ourselves missing it. But as we become used to focusing on Him whether sitting at His feet or doing His work, we can become free. We do not need to carry the false guilt of being imperfect conduits of Jesus' love. As we look to Him, He carries the responsibility both for creating resulting fruit and for continuing to develop us.

PAUSE & CONSIDER

- ❑ Consider a time when I know that the Lord worked through me as I served. How important was it that I was aware of the specific fruit He was harvesting? What does that suggest?

Redirecting focus

Doing what Jesus did by revealing the Father means we direct people's attention likewise. That's tricky in worship-arts ministry because by default we often draw attention towards ourselves.

Jesus plainly stated His reason for accomplishing "greater things" fruit through His people: *"so that the Father may be glorified in the Son"* (John 14:13). Uninterested in drawing glory to Himself, Jesus focused firmly upon the Father.

It makes sense that we should have the same attitude. But how can we direct attention anywhere unless some of it first comes to us?

That challenge faces worship folks every time we step on the platform, pick up an instrument, open our mouths, or push a knob.

Additionally, our "look at me!" culture practically trains everyone around us to exalt performing artists as people to be noticed, admired, and followed. Succumbing to a "bigger than life" mentality makes artists and technicians even greater magnets for attention.

Perhaps you have seen worship musicians take the opposite approach by trying to hide from any attention. I appreciate that they don't want to steal holy glory. They're exemplifying a great value, and I agree wholeheartedly. But I've found that congregations usually need leading, especially as our culture becomes less and less churched. Direction is helpful. It's hard to imagine someone successfully leading when they can't be seen or heard.

Hiding says we're copping out on revealing the Father.

Have you ever walked into a restaurant when there's no one to greet you, and no sign instructs you to seat yourself or to wait for assistance? It's awkward. I feel immediately out of place and self-conscious. It tells me that only those who already know the ropes actually belong; I'm neither expected nor wanted. The management has failed to provide what's necessary for me to enjoy the experience I came to have. Even if I do stay, I'll probably never return.

We sometimes need direction, especially in unfamiliar territory. So I hold a different viewpoint regarding handling attention. Instead of hiding the light of my leading, I want people to see Jesus through me. That starts by their looking in my direction. Then we can look to Jesus together.

When thinking about worship, embrace the challenge of being imitators of Christ. I want everything I *do* and all the time I *be* to become conduits for pointing people to the Lord.

This is my personal checklist:

- ❏ my skills
- ❏ my words
- ❏ where I look
- ❏ the smile on my face
- ❏ my body language
- ❏ the attitude I convey while in the seats or backstage
- ❏ my preparation
- ❏ my relationships
- ❏ the space around me (environment)
- ❏ literally everything

That doesn't mean I'm going to be comfortable. It just means I'm going to be a more malleable and successful leader.

We are worship reflectors. We *direct worship beyond ourselves toward Jesus.*

Then Jesus does what He does best, and directs worship to the Father.

PAUSE & CONSIDER_____

- ❏ What stands out to me in this chapter and why?

6.3 LIGHTS ALONG THE PATH

In the United States, the goal in football is simple: end every game with more points that the other team.

Success is obvious. Large H-shaped goal posts at the ends of the field remove any doubt about the direction players need to move the ball. Yard lines and 10-yard markers indicate progress along the way. A large scoreboard keeps everyone informed. The fans cheer for each forward step.

Everyone wants to win, but even when starting with a clear understanding of the objective, the game's intense excitement can disorient the players. The continual struggle with the opposition may deteriorate confidence and shake their will to push forward. Teams losing focus can struggle and fragment. They seldom win.

I've come to believe that the same is true in music ministry. Successful teams know where they're heading and that they're moving forward. They combine a primary goal with helpful waypoints and effective evaluation.

Your team can either flounder or flourish.

Losing our way

When people cannot find their way, the results can be devastating. This became so clear to me while I was transitioning between worship positions and making a living by installing home security systems. I learned that most people who die in home fires are not killed by flames. The real danger is the smoke. It impairs breathing and clouds the rooms and hallways. Navigation becomes extremely difficult, particularly amidst the confusion of a fire.

Tragically, sometimes people die only because they can't find a nearby exit. Today's technology detects fires earlier, but now we can even save lives by programming an illuminated path through the danger to safety.

Dangerous confusion easily occurs in ministry. Although teammates desire the same goal, differing tasks can make it seem like we play on completely different fields. We pull apart when the path toward the goal grows fuzzy.

We have to know where to go and how to get there.

It's easy to lose one's way in the midst of worship-arts ministry. It's also dangerous—what we do touches people's eternity.

Finding our way

In music ministry, we need regular reminders of our Romans 12:1-2 end goal of offering ourselves as full-self sacrifices of worship to the Lord. That goal must direct all we do. Additionally, clarifying points along the way can help us visualize what it means to serve successfully in our team role as we take our next step forward.

Specific details and methods vary from one church music program to another. Regardless, spelling out personal and group expectations dispels confusion. It helps each of us fulfill our role. We engage more confidently and influence better. We create appealing distraction-free environments as we dwell in the Lord's presence. We offer effective invitations to engage with the Lord as we express together Who He is and what He does.

Clear goals and waypoint markers protect us from becoming distracted, squandering resources, and losing our way. They help us survive the fires of ministry.

Serving-Related confusion

In music ministry, we often create good-but-contradictory messages:

- We perform... but we're not performers.

- We lead... we serve... we get out of the way.

- We arrive early... we leave late... we steward our time... we give our time away.

- We're relational... we're individualistic.

- We model authentic worship... we don't want to draw attention to ourselves.

- We're creative... we plan, prepare, and practice... we're spontaneous... we're deliberate.

- We embrace the passion and carry the fire... we quiet our souls beside still waters and call for rain.

- We celebrate... we pause and reflect.

- We seek excellence... we offer our humble gifts.

- We teach... we learn... we experience.

- We value simplicity... we use incredibly complex structures and equipment.

- We draw from the past... "be" in the now... and look to the future.

Sometimes our attempts to clarify simply cloud the way.

Waypoints to guide

The solution is to set out waypoints that help our minds focus on the task at hand without losing track of our big goal. Creating waypoints is like how a golfer lines up a putt shot by choosing a nearby point in line with the cup rather than aiming at the hole itself. Waypoints intentionally align individuals or teams with their end goal by providing reachable smaller nearby steps along the path.

I provided many waypoints as a worship pastor. They did not always help us move forward. Some were poorly designed or simply blurted without thinking. Many were weakly communicated. When I first started leading teams, I simply assumed that people who were passionate and skilled would have similar waypoints to those I set for myself. You can guess my results.

I'd like to think that you can do better.

You don't have to be a team leader to create and follow up on your own waypoint challenges. Consider sharing your challenge with a friend. Teammates can cheer one another on and evaluate success together. Waypoints can be excellent team builders.

Good waypoints:

- Clarify the *who, when* and *where* of a task.

- Create forward movement toward the goalpost.

- Specify the *how* of a task while allowing for the appropriate amount of flexibility and initiative.

- Challenge the team or individual to stretch without overreaching or setting up failure.

- Provide an out if necessary.

- Specify a clear, measurable result.

- Allow for 2-way communication to clarify and confirm expectations or questions.

Example of an individual waypoint challenge by the worship leader:

"John, this coming Sunday, I'd like you to prepare the 8-bar lead guitar solo for our opening song. This will be a good way to freshen the song as we invite the congregation to engage. *You can either follow the example posted online or play the melody. Sue usually plays the intro on keys, but I think you can handle this even though it may stretch you. If some coaching would be helpful after you've had a chance to work on it, I can meet with you Tuesday before team practice. If you're not going to be able to take this on, please let me know by Tuesday morning so I can give Sue time to prepare. Are you up to the challenge?"*

185

Example of a team waypoint challenge by the worship leader:

"This week as a team, let's work on our grand pauses. Let's hit all three grand pauses in the set precisely and follow them with a massive and perfectly timed next chord—both musically and with our body language. I know tightening these highlights will open up those moments for the congregation. Can we do that?"

Example of a personal waypoint challenge by a team member:

"This week I want to work on how I express worship while I'm not singing. I'll select four places in the set when I have no vocal responsibilities and focus on breaking out of my comfort zone by using my face, arms, and body to show Jesus my praise to Him. Then I can review the video playback with a friend to see if others may have been impacted by what I communicated."

PAUSE & CONSIDER

❑ What one thing can I stretch in this week, what risk can I take in which I will surely fall flat unless the Lord steps in and helps me grow?

6.4 MEASURING STICKS

It's not enough to simply have good, intentional waypoints. You must communicate them and you must verify when they've been reached or missed.

The saying goes, "People don't know what they don't know." Communicate your waypoints through whatever form works *effectively* for your teammates. You may use ministry team handbooks, one-on-one reviews, printed station guidelines, emails/texts, scheduling software, YouTube videos, group discussions, sticky-notes posted by team members, team workshops, or another alternative.

> *Every person serving in every role should be able to envision clearly what their successfully fulfilled role will look like.*

Then—and this is *absolutely* vital—pause at appropriate intervals to assess together how you're doing.

In football, sometimes the referees need to clarify if a team has made enough progress to earn the opportunity to continue to move the ball. Forward movement is evaluated by bringing out a measurement chain. This 100 year old tradition clarifies for everyone the exact location of the ball in relationship to its starting position.

Similarly, in music ministry, we need methods to signal whether we've reached our waypoint challenges. These "measuring sticks" are values-based tools that provide a baseline for interpreting success.

The tricky part isn't *having* measuring sticks. Everyone has them. The tricky part is having *good* measuring sticks.

You can easily identify your collection of measuring sticks. Imagine this discussion:

Someone asks, "How'd it go on team today?"

You say, "Great!"

They inquire, "Why?"

You respond, "Well..."

Everything following the "Well..." part of your answer reveals what matters to you. You may include how effectively you accomplished your role, particular response by certain people, a gut feeling, avoidance of an irritation, the balance of the sound in your ears, a mistake, noticing someone humming one of your songs while leaving the building, the volume of the congregational singing, or even how your hair looked on the confidence monitor. For better or worse, your measuring sticks show.

PAUSE & CONSIDER_____

❑   What does one of my measuring sticks
    that influences me significantly say
    about what matters to me in ministry?

When measuring sticks go wrong

Although everyone has their own set of measuring sticks, not every measuring stick may be helpful.

Have you ever thought this in the midst of worship? "Hey, God, things are going great! The worship feels so intense. The team is tight and the people are engaged. You must be moving!" Yet after the busyness fades, you can't shake a nagging suspicion that perhaps God wasn't in the excitement after all. But in the moment it felt so good.

Or did you ever finish a set just feeling flat? Blah. Then someone came up beaming because they encountered God in a life-changing moment, and they just had to let you know. Eternity came down and you missed it.

Maybe sometimes we simply use the wrong measuring stick.

Doing so can have dire consequences on an eternal scale. The Bible records a sobering example of failed measuring sticks in Matthew 25:31-46 when Jesus described how He will separate His sheep from the goats. What's crazy is that each group measures themselves by the other group's measuring stick, and neither group realizes that their measuring sticks are faulty. The sheep don't even realize that they were taking care of Jesus, and the goats have no clue that they are heading toward eternal punishment.

In an earlier passage (Matthew 7:21-23), Jesus tells about a large group of religious people with a truly amazing list of accomplishments. See how you measure up:

❑ They identify themselves as believers and call Jesus "Lord."

❑ They boldly declared truths of God and call people to repentance in Jesus' name.

❑ They successfully help people by driving out demons in Jesus' name.

❑ They perform many other miracles in Jesus' name.

Whatever your doctrinal stance, you can acknowledge that these folks have something significant going on. Jesus didn't question the miracles' authenticity. And while we may be a bit apprehensive about attending one of their services, we'd be curious, if not outright wowed—I'm sure it would be something to see. But Jesus isn't impressed. Just the opposite. He said that rather than doing the will of His Father, they actually do evil, and that He *never* knew them.

Talk about having a wrong measuring stick!

These people accomplish some impressive results—things that Jesus Himself did, things that He told His disciples to do, things He said that other people who follow Him would do. As far as actions were concerned, these folks look like things are going powerfully well. But that isn't the whole story.

They capture the form, yet totally miss the person of Jesus.

The bad fruit in their lives is far more foundational to Him. He calls us to walk with Him, but these folks totally miss the boat. Literally. Jesus said they'll be cut down and thrown in the fire. Can we dare ignore the significance?

We must apply good measuring sticks. If we cannot correctly gage whether we're following the True Wind, can we know that we point those in our care in the right direction? Can we trust that we're not mistaking excitement for Jesus?

Worship teams usually work incredibly hard. Before a set, the team and leader prepare their best praise offering from their resources of time, creativity, energy, gifts, equipment, passion, etc. Then during the set they invite the congregation to join in, and together the church expresses their worship to the Lord. We need to that we use our gifts and resources well.

The measuring sticks we select either keep us blind or open our eyes.

PAUSE & CONSIDER_____

❑   What measuring stick could actually
    become a distraction for me?

6.5 BUILDING MEASURING STICKS

Wouldn't it be helpful if the Bible dictated for us a post-service check list? Jesus did promise the disciples that whoever believes in Him will do even greater works than they saw Jesus doing, and His list is incredibly impressive.

But, despite all the great things going on in churches all over the planet, I've yet to hear of a church where their Planning Center Online Service Schedule regularly lists:

9:15-9:15—Call to Worship, Pastor Ron

9:15am-9:23am—Raise the Dead...

> ...followed by some announcements, a brief prayer, an offering, and a 40 minute sermon.

Good measuring sticks allow you to acknowledge your progress, learn from failure, celebrate transformation, and restore your drive. They help you reevaluate and determine whether or not your investment of time, energy, resources, and so on effectively reaches toward the big goal.

How we measure determines how we improve by informing us when we've been successful. It creates an awareness of what we even mean by success. We become sensitive to success's symptoms. We anticipate accomplishing our goals, and more readily pay the price to get there. We catch the vision and better realize what it takes to accomplish that vision and step into the new.

> *With good measuring sticks, we more willingly declare to our leaders, "Yes, let's take the hill! Perhaps God will act on our behalf. You lead and I'll follow. I am with you, heart and soul."[21]*

Evaluating the results of our effort certainly is not about feelings. Many of us understand that the ultimate goal isn't about how well we played, how well we followed our plan, or how much the people's expressions and body movement suggested that they were engaged internally. And most worship people can usually agree that an important component of worship is that the Holy Spirit is actively at work in each person's life to draw them toward a more full interaction with God. But how do we measure *that*?

We will where I am convinced is the absolutely best place to start.

Scripture and fruit

Identifying the right measuring stick can be tricky. Even our own awareness can mislead us.

For example, recently at a family gathering my nephew brought out his Oculus virtual reality headgear and some new games. Actually, I think the real game was "let's put this on everyone over the age 40 and laugh at what they do." I obliged. As I donned the headgear, I was immediately immersed in the world of a wild west Dodge City shoot out. It was pretty amazing. But when I leaned forward to dodge from my opponents, I put my hand on a barrel to steady myself. Of course, there was no barrel. My hand passed through, followed by the rest of me. To everyone's amusement I ended up on the floor. It was a jarring reminder that my perceptions didn't align with true reality.

We need to trust a perspective more grounded than our own.

---

[21] I love how this response given by Prince Jonathan's armor bearer when asked to accept a nearly-suicidal mission turned the tide of war.

As our great designer, the Lord knows our need. A primary way He provides guidance is through scripture. King David wrote that the Lord's Word is a "lamp to my feet and a light to my path." He knew that God's grasp of reality is—of all things—stable.

I find that I must continually re-align, redefine, and evaluate my "success" by God's purposes and perspective rather than my own. I rediscover God's reminders that His ways and thoughts are always larger, deeper, and more encompassing than I can comprehend.

I want to understand what matters to the heart of Almighty God. I want to follow Jesus' example and be about my Father's business. So, at least for me, the best place to develop measuring sticks is looking to the scriptures and asking, "What does God say?"

If you want good value-based measuring sticks—I mean really good ones that will stoke the fires of your passion and crystallize your vision—don't borrow them from anyone else. Yes, you may gain helpful opinions from other people you respect, especially those who have gone where you hope to go, but remember that the Lord has a unique plan for you. Open the Book yourself. The Lord promised that His Holy Spirit will guide you. Seek that nudge. Although I'd gladly share my own list—many are imbedded within these pages— you're best served by starting at The Source.

Besides, you know your church culture. You know what they find meaningful. You know how God moves amongst you. You know what doors most readily open your hearts to truth. You are the person most qualified to discover the specific measuring sticks to accurately guide your church through scriptural guidelines. It's your responsibility.

Discovering the best measuring sticks requires an investment of time. I will never forget experiencing this firsthand when the church I attended divided into groups to search verse by verse through the entire Bible in order to identify the specific keys we needed to follow in order to move forward. We considered every single verse, all 31,102 of them. Although it took several months, our differing concepts and preconceptions clarified and melded into a crystal clear, unified vision.

Imagine what could happen if you and your team deliberately

implemented a checklist of values that you discover together in the Bible. It will change the way you function. It will transform attitudes. Think of the confidence that comes when you know what you do is based on what matters to Jesus and how He moves in your midst. You will become better conduits of what Jesus wants to impart. That's a fantastic place to start.

The Bible provides the kinds of measuring sticks that will grow with you. They will continually challenge you week after week without allowing things to slip. They maintain room to learn, grow, and transform.

PAUSE & CONSIDER_____

❑ What scripture passage stands out to me as offering insight into what really matters regarding serving in my role in worship-arts ministry?

6.6 IMPLEMENTING MEASURING STICKS

Once your deliberate, value-based measuring sticks are identified, you can ask how the results of your services compare to your measuring sticks. Consider focusing on the impact that occurs through activities rather than on the activities themselves.

- If Jesus walked in on your service or rehearsal, would He be pleased?

- Do the congregation's hearts and minds better align with His words and tone?

- Do people leave your time together more deeply in love with Him?

- Are they pointed toward the Father?

- Are they turning from their sins?

- Do they become less afraid?

- Do they take up the light, easy yoke and burden of Jesus?

- Are they exhorted to go out and share Jesus' good news with others?

- Do they experience less of themselves and more of Jesus?

- Do those who serve reflect Jesus' attitude of love?

Because you cannot read the hearts of your congregation, these questions may be difficult to answer. It helps if you are willing to ask and if they're willing to tell you honestly.

But you do know your own heart. So when asking such questions, start with yourself.

How can you adjust to become more effective?

Your ministry's ability to reach your goal will be either limited or enabled by the measuring stick you choose and how you implement it.

Twice Jesus said in Matthew 7 that we can judge by fruit (verses 16 and 20). He promises in John 12 that if we abide in Him, we will bear fruit. Is the kind of fruit produced by your service the same kind that He produces? When you serve, is there an increase in love? Joy? Peace? Patience and kindness? Gentleness and goodness? Are you now more faithful? Have you become more self-controlled? In short, are you more like Jesus through serving?

If such fruit is being cultivated in your own life, there's a pretty clear indicator that the Lord will be shining through you. When those you serve also choose to abide in Jesus' love, they'll experience similar fruit. Even if you can't see or hear it, Jesus said your fruit will grow. Identifying fruit gives us a chance to adjust our course or celebrate becoming more Christ-like.

Here's an example of applying a value-based measuring stick to a waypoint.

Suppose you base a measuring stick upon Jesus' directive in John 4:23-24 to worship in spirit and in truth. We'll call this your Authenticity measuring stick. Let's say that your waypoint challenge is to express your joy more while playing your instrument. Afterwards, applying your measuring stick may lead you to ask yourself whether you felt stretched in sacrificially offering up your pride. Perhaps you'll consider that by learning your part better, you may feel more free to physically express your joy by smiling instead of concentrating on the next chord change. This may lead you to create your next waypoint challenge of completely memorizing one song in the upcoming set so well that you can focus completely on physically expressing your worship.

PAUSE & CONSIDER_____

❑ How might I modify one of my measuring sticks to help me become more effective?

6.7 FOLLOWING UP BUILDS

Have you ever experienced a time when someone promised you something, but then failed to deliver? There you are, expectations raised, hopeful for something special, just to be let down. It's discouraging. It feels like you lost something or that something was stolen from you. You seem to matter less. It's natural after that to have diminished trust for the promiser, isn't it?

When you suggest a challenge to your team, you're really offering a promise. If they agree, they are accepting your deal, your bargain. They commit to an exchange of effort, preparation, or something from themselves in return for some kind of growth or result. As the team experiences a sense of reaching these goals successfully, they more willingly take up your next challenge. But if you fail to verify that the goal was reached, team members do not know whether their investment was squandered. Doubt lingers. Then, next time, instead of reaching farther, they'll reserve more of themselves from taking on the challenge. They'll either withhold or refrain altogether. All for the lack of knowledge.

Besides, confirming a successful exchange builds the desire for more. It establishes a culture of digging deep. Doing this in the presence of one another creates added value because, not only is the team challenged to experience similar growth, everyone gets to celebrate and confirm that someone had impact. Jesus was moving and He did it through a team member. How exciting!

So if you really want the team to grow, if you want momentum to build, you cannot ignore this step. Even in the rush of getting home or preparing for the next week, verify whether you met your waypoints.

And this needs to happen soon after the set. Or, like the ripples of a pebble dropped in water, the benefit fades away. Bloop... ripple... ripple... ripple... forgotten... lost.

So immediately following the set, whether sitting down for a short meeting, grabbing a quick drink at the water fountain, or making a conference call on the way to lunch, allow opportunity for others on your team to share successes, failures, and observations.

Here are 3 quick debrief questions:

1. What did you sense God doing? (including the days leading to the set)

2. What worked?

3. What may need addressing?

These questions open an opportunity to celebrate how He moved in us, to thank Him for allowing us to be part of His work, and to double check both our hearts and the measuring sticks we use to evaluate what was accomplished.

I really value meeting with my team after a set to unpack their stories and observations. We acknowledge our areas of needed growth. It helps us trust that God is doing His work, even if it either remained unseen or unfolded differently than we anticipated. We're trying to take His promises at face value, understand that He accomplishes His goals for the day, and be grateful that He has called us to play a part in gathering His harvest.

Such discussion provides opportunity to repackage and address when teammates miss the mark. Obviously, no one wants a "here's how you messed up and should have done better" lecture. How you communicate helps others decide whether to risk failure in the future. Tread lightly. Besides, most of us who value worship expression already know our blunders. You can help your people see the value in making their attempt. Learning from our blunders softens the sting and shares the lesson. While failure matters (or else it wouldn't be worth the risk), it is worth celebrating that a team member made the attempt in the first place. It builds a culture of embracing deliberate growth. We try again. Learning from failure brings something valuable to everyone—if we're willing to be humble.

Debriefing serves to remind you and the team that, yes, the plan you envisioned, the path you led, was successful. Or, even if it failed, you survived to learn something that will make the next hill easier to climb. It creates a culture that values growth and celebrates when people deliberately embrace transformation. It honors your big goal and your waypoints. It validates your measuring sticks. It frees you to get back to work with the confidence that you are keeping the main thing the main thing.

Debriefing reveals, honors, and celebrates what God is doing.

When debriefing with the team isn't possible, I like to send notes that recognize successes. I have a stack of Thank You post cards on my desk—I do the artwork myself—upon which I can jot down "you made a difference" observations. I keep comments as short and simple as possible. They must be earned. (Most people know when a complement feels undeserved, and while someone may appreciate the effort, it doesn't build trust.) The postcards get posted within a day or two of the set, and wow, are they appreciated! I hear about them, I get thanked for them, and I've seen them still stuck to refrigerator doors over a year later.

Whether you lead or not, you can be an important encourager simply by recognizing when people succeed in what matters to them.

The evaluation step is vitally important. Goal setting without a follow up is worse than wasted energy because it practically guarantees resistance to making future investments in growth. The positives of reinforcing success, recognizing fruit, and celebrating growth are some of the most motivating dynamics out there. If you want to grow a culture of positive growth, meet to apply your measuring sticks.

❑ If I could ask someone else to evaluate
    my serving by only one measuring stick,
    what would it be?

You're one of the team

Don't forget to include yourself when creating waypoint challenges and measuring sticks!

Surely you wouldn't ask anything of others that you wouldn't do yourself. Regardless of how good you are, how mature, how experienced, at some point the rest of the team will see you struggle and fail. Just like everyone else, you're in transformation. By allowing others to see you grow, you communicate emphatically that everyone learns. And if you're learning, they have permission to learn, too. Besides, recognizing when you miss the mark models humility and embracing challenge. Why withhold?

You may even find that the rest of the team's willingness to take risks allows you to push yourself farther.

It's an excellent recipe for success. Identify your goalpost. Clarify the path with good waypoints. Measure your success. Repeat. Flourish.

DOING YOUR PART BETTER

7.0 MORE

We want to be relevant to those we're trying to impact. But it's hard to stay current. And even though our end goal is a life of sacrificial worship, it's difficult to invite others to do the same when our mode of communication has lost its relevance.

"Contemporary" means existing in the present. By default, it seems that anyone serving in contemporary music ministry who slows down for a second immediately faces cultural and technical obsolescence, and that's if the person was ever up to speed in the first place.

The longer a person serves, the more likely they will run into this struggle. It often takes us by surprise. Perhaps you've seen this happen yourself.

It poses quite a dilemma. On one hand, we desire to communicate relevantly amidst continual changes in technology, styles, and technique. In our "It's gotta be new and it's gotta be now" culture, just keeping current can be overwhelming. On the other hand, we desire to focus on meeting a spiritual need that remains as gaping as when we first grabbed the apple in the garden. The deadly temptation is to let go of one goal or the other.

I think this dilemma is great!

It's great because God, in His genius, knew that our temptation to become complacent is the immature side of our being content in all things.

In His grace, He built reminders into our maturing process to nudge us forward. He gifted us with creativity and a desire for discovery. He made us hungry for more. It's why the Bible says in Lamentations 3:22-23 that His loving compassion is new every morning. It's why at least seven times the Old and New Testaments instruct us about singing a new song to the Lord.

Keep reaching.

If what I bring to the altar honors the Lord, as I grow, so too grows what I can bring. I want my offering to be greater. So I must never stop developing.

Jesus likes us to grow, too. I think He expects it.

It's interesting that in Jesus' parable of the talents in Matthew 25:14-30, the first action taken by the ruler of the two successful servants is to tally the return they each presented on his investment.

Whether he initially gave them a one, two, or five talent gift, they were personally responsible that it produced results. As long as they produced results, the ruler was pleased. After rewarding them, he commanded them to go out and become even more fruitful.[22]

Did you notice that none of the servants in Jesus' parable compared their return with the others? That's hard to do in our culture. Awards and competitions constantly teach us to measure ourselves by the artistic expressions and achievements of others.

Sometimes our roles require that we evaluate one another's skills.

- Team leaders select which voice best matches a part.

---

[22] The only exception was the servant who withheld his talent from the risk of exposure. I wonder how many people dare sharing his fate by failing to use what the Lord has invested in them.

- Sound techs decide which channel to increase or lower to help team blend.

- Band directors audition potential members to evaluate skill sets and determine the most appropriate way for that person to have effective impact.

- Musicians can identify strengths in one another from which they can learn and expand their own skill toolbox.

These are all ways of valuing one another and the gifts the Lord has instilled.

We may need to reign ourselves in to avoid stepping into destructive comparisons by equating skill level with personal value.

Jesus didn't say whether or not the servants in His parable compared either their initial gift, their results, or their reward. Perhaps the 5-talent guy congratulated the 2-talent guy on his result. In real life, everyone would know.

This parable reminds me that we don't need to evaluate ourselves and our fruit based upon the skills and results that other people have.

But we do need to consider how to best produce the greatest return on the Lord's investment in us.

Perhaps it's like how goldfish only grow as large as their environment allows. They stop getting bigger once they've maximized their size for the space. Place them in a bigger container, and they continue growing. Likewise, if we give up reaching for the new, we're stuck in yesterday.

Thankfully, the Lord gives me little opportunity to think that I've arrived. It seems like every time I think I reach the top of my game, He reminds me of my glaring need for more. Maybe you've experienced a similar nudge to fly the warm nest of "I'm satisfied."

Jesus rewards us with the opportunity to add to the crown that we'll eventually place at His feet in glory. I don't want to settle for the crown that currently awaits me. I want to give Him more! But I'm maxed out. Everything in me has led up to my current result. To give more, I must become more.

❑ What does my willingness to spend my limited resources of time, energy, and money to expand my skill toolbox say about how I value increasing the return on the Lord's investment in me?

7.1 HOLY DISSATISFACTION

I'd rather not share the following example with you. It's worse than embarrassing. It reminds me of how small my perspective can be. But it illustrates that every time I reached a new level of impact, it wasn't long before something happened to show that I needed to grow more. Perhaps you can relate.

Here's what I did.

About 3 decades ago I began serving as a volunteer worship leader at my church. The following 7 years I threw myself into creating significant worship experiences, sometimes spending 40 hours a week on top of my day job. I felt good about it because every week I led, everything seemed to come together. We all agreed—the pastor, the team, the congregation—everyone called it a success, including me.

Eventually I took a music director staff position at another church. About six months later I ran into a musician from my previous church. After chatting a bit, he confided, "We've never been able to play like when you were with us." He meant that as a complement, but his words helped me realize that once I was gone, so was my impact.

That harsh realization reminds me of the engraving on the tomb of one of England's greatest poets—John Keats. I've seen his dying words—they're carved into his headstone. "Here lies one whose name was writ in water." He feared that after he passed on, the ripples of his life would smooth away, forgotten.

I had done the same thing. I merely taught reliance. I had accomplished my vision, but without even realizing it, I failed to take them beyond myself. Splash—bloop—gone.

I never wanted to fail like that again.

So at my new music director position, I expanded my vision by making sure that the musicians and technicians learned *why* and *how* to get where we wanted to go. I reached my goal. They got it.

I eventually accepted a worship pastor position at what grew into one of the largest multi-site congregations in that part of the state. One day I got a phone call.

He said, "I've held your old worship director position for about a year. I want you to know that I so appreciate how you've trained the team. I don't know how you did it, but I never need to explain what to do—they already know. I'm just amazed. Thank you." After talking a bit more he admitted, "Honestly I am tired. I feel alone—I can't get anyone to give me a break by filling my spot."

Since I'm a problem solver, I immediately began considering their roster and the skills they had developed. Suddenly the realization struck me that in 4 years, even with the right people, I failed to develop a single worship leader. The opportunity hadn't even crossed my mind. Once again I found that although I succeeded in my vision, I failed at something bigger.

So at the multi-site church I expanded my vision by developing worship leaders for our campuses, enough that we had multiple leaders to fill each of our slots and some even went to serve elsewhere. My failure there was that I didn't do enough to connect and help other churches develop. This has led me to expand my vision, and now I partner with church teams and leaders to increase their impact. And I still need to grow!

Although I'm passionate about having impact, my definition of what that means keeps expanding.

I continually measure what I do. My wife Anita kindly refers to my obsession as "Holy Dissatisfaction." I celebrate accomplishment, but I'm also learning to leverage big failure to expand my vision and remain open to continued growth.

Vision inevitably fails. Each time I set out to succeed, I had no clue that my goal was too small. Eventually someone paid the price for my limited vision—usually the very people I was giving my all to serve.

I've had the opportunity to meet worship musicians and technicians from all over the world. We all want to be successful in our role. We pay a price to succeed—time, energy, resources. But success stalls when we've met our benchmarks and fail to raise the bar.

Don't settle for your impact fading away, being writ on water. Utilize "Holy Dissatisfaction" and continually raise your bar by expanding your vision. A big fail can light the way toward growth.

We must grow. And to do that, we must remain teachable.

PAUSE & CONSIDER_____

❑ As I look back on my experiences, how has one of my greatest successes revealed a need for new growth?

7.2 LEARNING FROM OTHERS

In addition to the constant uphill climb, we're also surrounded by other people who always seem to be at least one step ahead. Sometimes they make everything look so easy.

There're the ones who force me to do an attitude check.

Ever hear this?

"No matter the size of the pond, there's always a bigger fish."

I suspect it's true, at least where music and tech are concerned. There's no shortage of talent. Someone inevitably comes along who knows more, plays better, has better gear, or just looks way cooler.

But comparison can grow into jealousy. Until I learned to handle my attitude, when around people having skills that eclipsed my own, I could drifting into one of the following damaging responses.

- Tear them down in my mind by finding faults
- Seek a new piece of gear or a technique to close the gap
- Surround myself with people having skills I could outdo
- Stew and becoming depressed
- Give up and settle for "I'm as good as I'll ever be, outdated and irrelevant."

None of that is healthy.

It's humbling. But joy comes when I realize that as long as I'm giving my all and serving well, the Lord has my skill set just where it needs to be.

This frees me to turn "competitors" into mentors I can learn from and appreciate.

I find that I always learn when working with players more skilled than myself. I love picking the brains of people who have already tried out tools I've been curious to demo. And it's an honor to play with world class musicians, even when I'm weakest one on the platform—not only does their playing makes me sound better than I am, but I become better!

It's not only the truly top people who help me learn. Cultivating a more healthy attitude toward others has helped me receive from anyone, including picking up tricks and tips from people who are just starting out.

> *As long as I keep the "I should be teaching them" blinders out of my mind, there's always something new I can pick up.*

The same is probably true for you.

That's because none of us have arrived yet. There's always more to learn, another tool to add to the toolbox, another nuance for making our part shine just a little more.

Just good enough

Having a "there's more to help me improve my impact" attitude also keeps us from falling into the danger of settling for stagnation.

Not long after I picked up a guitar for the first time at age 14, I met a real-life professional guitarist. He played in dance bands. I was so impressed. I asked for a tip. Here is his sage wisdom: "If you're having a bad night and aren't playing well, just crank up the volume. The audience will never know. It's good enough for rock 'n roll."

That's one bit of advice I've never followed.

Sometimes there is a temptation for those who serve in worship-arts ministry to behave as if we believed that what we are doing is good enough for church worship music. Striving for *better* is unnecessary. We fall into the trap of being just good enough.

It's like the old summer camp skit. From the distance you hear a hound dog howling mournfully. One by one, each of the family is asked to go check on Ol' Blue. No one is willing. Everyone complains of being "just too tired to move." Finally someone sighs, gets up, shuffles out, and eventually returns. Ol' Blue's problem? He's sitting on a cactus and just too tired to move.

Perhaps we're sitting on the same cactus.

Maybe it's time to get up.

PAUSE & CONSIDER_____

❑   What is the most daunting challenge I
     fear to face if I embrace my next area
     of significant growth?

7.3 GIVING YOUR EYES AND EARS

Have you ever felt in music ministry that everyone wants a piece of you and there's not enough to go around?

Many voices call for our attention. Leaders expect us to follow their instructions. Teammates expect us to coordinate our role with theirs. The congregation looks to us for direction. We have to authentically engage our own selves personally. The Lord deserves our focus and attention. The Holy Spirit seeks to guide and comfort us. Each of these areas of focus have scripturally legitimate considerations.

This forces a difficult choice. We can decide to focus *internally* on self-reflection or interaction with the Holy Spirit dwelling in us. Instead, we may focus *externally* on the those around us. Or we could simply shut down all interaction and focus solely on the task of making music.

Having the wrong focus may cause us inadvertently to miss something important.

So who gets our attention?

We're probably never going to agree on one singular focus. The Bible doesn't either.

- John 17:1 says that a focus glorifying Jesus glorifies God, so glorifying Jesus should be our focus.

- Romans 15:6 says that the Church should focus on glorifying the Father.

- Matthew 18:20 reveals the importance of gathering together as a body, so that should be our focus.

- 1 Corinthians 11:28 says we need to examine ourselves, and that's necessary to the John 4:23 passage in which Jesus emphasized worshiping in spirit and in truth. So we must focus on our own hearts.

- John 14:26 says the Holy Spirit will guide us, so that should be our focus.

- Ephesians 6:12 says that we address spiritual forces, so that should be our focus.

- James 1:27 says that true religious activity is caring for widows and orphans, so social justice should be our focus.

- Psalm 150 commands loud expressions of praise, so that should be our focus. Pass out the cowbells and tambourines!

You can keep adding to the list. I'm oversimplifying these important passages, but here's my point: Each focus has a legitimate place during our congregational times of expressing worship. God uses each of these to meet with each of us simultaneously, both individually and as a group.

We're often each left to create our own balance of where to look and what to contemplate as we identify our specific audience.

That can be particularly challenging for me. On one hand my mind tends to focus on one thing at a time and forget everything else, like a horse harnessed with blinders. On the other hand, my artsy self loves seeing the whole picture and how each focus of praise entwines together to weave a worship tapestry honoring the Lord. Trying to simultaneously multi-task each focus can be overwhelming.

We don't need to be paralyzed by options.

In reality, during a set I find my focus flittering from one thing to another. But if I just wing it, I can miss the mark, too, and leave

215

behind either the congregation, the team, or my own heart.

Being the deliberate person I am, preplanning my focus helps point my heart, mind, and body in the right direction. Because worship is interactive and dynamic, I try to remain flexible. But while I adapt when something may rightfully rise up to draw my attention, I know my bases are covered. For me that's a great starting place.

If you're wondering what my process looks like, here's an example. As I look through an upcoming set, I prayerfully identify moments that offer special opportunities for each area of focus. Whether I'm leading or simply part of a musical or technical team, I consider when it's important to use words or body language to invite the congregation to engage or help them transition. Identifying when I know the congregation and team will not need interaction with me permits focusing wholly on expressing my heart to Jesus. I look for when to be particularly sensitive to the Holy Spirit's guidance. I ask at what points I need to express what arises from interaction with the Lord, such as repenting, sharing my heart, or addressing spiritual realities. I mark when the team and I may need reminders about where to go next musically. Then as the set actually unfolds, I follow my planned focus unless the Lord directs otherwise.

For me, being deliberate enables freedom. That way I connect where, when, how, and with whom I need to. Expectantly anticipating the Lord's move readies my heart and mind to respond.

My approach is not for everyone. It would completely hamper my wife! She would much rather think of congregational times as an unfolding conversation in which everyone interactively expresses their hearts to Jesus together. That approach works well for her. Our varying approaches allow us each to reach different places in worship. (That's one benefit in churches having multiple worship leaders.)

Isn't that variety awesome!

So rather than create a cookie-cutter formula for everyone, let's consider the seven primary areas of attention—call them audience partners—as you create your own focus balance.

Audience Partner: Leaders — What section leader, conductor, worship leader, pastor, or other person do you need to follow? Are there key moments when you need to be specifically aware of changes or moments of direction? How can you communicate support to encourage them?

Audience Partner: Congregation — When might the congregation specifically benefit from your actions or words? Are there key transitions during which you can focus others' attention appropriately? How can you best communicate nonverbally through your body language and facial expressions? Are there specific people who you might connect with in a meaningful way? How can you effectively understand what others are experiencing? How can you be praying for them during key moments?

Audience Partner: Teammates — When can you encourage your teammates? How can you pray for them, support them, or free their focus? What information do you need to communicate to clarify roles or remind one another about details?

Audience Partner: Self — When can you express your heart without concerning yourself with other details? Who can you entrust to "watch the shop" so that you can freely focus internally at a particular point? What business with God do you need to address beforehand to be free from baggage or distractions?

Audience Partner: Holy Spirit — Can you quiet other details so that you can better interact with the Holy Spirit's prompting? Are there key moments when you need to particularly focus or be free to respond to how the Holy Spirit is guiding you in your own life? Can someone trustworthy confirm what you sense?

Audience Partner: Jesus — When are appropriate times to specifically declare and celebrate what the Lord is doing in your own life or intimately share your own love and devotion with Him? How can you refocus your own attention toward the Lord? Who can you rely upon to temporarily cover your role so you can focus here?

Audience Partner: Other Spiritual Realities — When and how can you address this? Are there specific scriptures or truths of God that need to be declared at a particular point? Is there some action or musical arrangement that will communicate what may need to be declared? (While churches approach this point very differently, both the Old and New Testaments demonstrate the appropriateness of declaring to everyone in both the physical and spiritual realms that the Lord of Hosts is at hand and that nothing can stand before Him.)

Audience Partner: None — Sometimes we may face a particularly difficult task requiring our full attention. How can you free yourself at such times from another focus? How can you return to an appropriate focus once that moment passes?

There are many things to think about. No wonder we find it a challenge! One of the great keys is realizing that at particular times we must focus on particular things. Then we can involve others to free us so that we can address it appropriately and free from distraction.

PAUSE & CONSIDER_____

❑ What can I do to more regularly maintain a focus that is very important and necessary to me?

7.4 WE

No one promised that serving would be easy. At least no one ever told me that it would be. Good thing—they'd have been lying. But I never realized that one of the greatest challenges deals with remembering that I'm ministering in the first place.

We perform a technically-challenging role. We simultaneously personally worship the Lord while also directing the focus of others towards Him. Because we serve within the context of a community that the Lord designed specifically for meeting people's needs, we also seek to reflect Jesus and represent Him to the world outside our church walls.

That's one tricky job description! Even if we're learning to maintain balance between our own internal and external areas of focus, it can be challenging to bring the congregation along.

> *Not only do we expect the congregation to observe our worship and be in mental agreement, we expect them to participate.*

Getting them to join in with us is a big reason we serve. But sometimes it seems that they don't want to cooperate. Perhaps we simply fail to connect.

Performance and individualism

Perhaps we don't feel that we need congregational engagement. I admit that sometimes I prefer my solitary "closet" worship experience with the Lord. I enjoy the process of playing with other musicians and techs. I love making music! When I perform for my own personal satisfaction like this, it can feel like the congregation is merely along for the ride.

It's worth reminding ourselves that musicians play a very important role in our larger culture. Music performances reinforce values, express emotions, raise awareness, connect communities, and entertain. These purposes matter. But they're not our primary intent when we use the phrase "expressing worship."

Have you ever experienced when a church band treats the congregation like mere observers? How easily do you engage with the Lord when people approach music at church like a form of Christian karaoke? They may help focus our thoughts on truths about God. But this so easily misses the restorative reason for the cross. Jesus desires our full participation, not just our mental assent. Without cultivating engagement, we may miss having the impact on others that He called us to accomplish by serving in the first place.

Considering the extent of scripture's worship focus, Jesus knew we musicians and technicians may lose sight of His other priorities. We can become susceptible to worshiping the activities and tools of worship. In our self-focused culture, we may simply forget about people around us or even the One we're supposedly worshiping. We can become absorbed by our own interaction with God, by the process of creating expressions of worship, or by getting lost exploring what we discover within our own hearts.

It can be so easy for us to ignore everyone else in the room.

The people factor

But congregational worship is meant to be a shared experience.

It's like Jesus reminding the disciples to let go of the business at hand in order to allow the children to approach Him (Matthew 19:14, Mark 10:14, Luke 18:16).

The Bible says in Mark 12:33:

"To love him with all your heart, with all your understanding and with all your strength, and to love your neighbor as yourself is more important than all burnt offerings and sacrifices."

Jesus identifies two things more important than church activities. Did you catch them? Worship with our full self, and that bit about our neighbor.

> ***Our connection with others is more important to Jesus than our expressions of worship. Jesus is reminding us to keep our priorities straight and not get so caught up in our expressions and sacrificial offerings that we tread upon loving others His way.***

He didn't design expressions of praise to end when we close our mouths. Worship is not merely a solo activity. Jesus deliberately includes others, and wants us to do the same.

Most of us serving as church musicians or technicians are not starry-eyed hopefuls trying to establish our music performance careers. By far most church teams desire to share with the congregation a mutually engaged expression of corporate praise. It's awesome when we succeed.

PAUSE & CONSIDER_____

❑ What might be a good warning flag to signal to myself that my approach to serving may miscommunicate a lack of Jesus' love?

7.5 AVENUES FOR CONNECTION

For those of us who don't talk directly to the congregation during a worship set, it may be tempting to ignore connecting with them.

Doing so misses a powerful opportunity.

Talking is overrated. Powerful communication occurs even when our mouths are closed. Perhaps you've heard the Connection Impact Rule state that of what we communicate, 55% comes through body language, 35% through the attitude we convey, and only 10% through the actual words we may use. Regardless of whether you are on or off the platform, your opportunity to impact remains.

Whether in a technical or a musical role, we each can help the congregation engage. Missing one of these five avenues forfeits an opportunity. Consider how developing your role reduces a potential distraction or extends an avenue to connect.

1. **Environment** — *We create a space in which the senses engage*

    Visual: your body language, gestures, expressions, outfit and stage position, projected images, typos, lighting, stage proximity, line of sight obstructions, eye contact, aesthetics, visibility of lyrics, video quality, cleanliness, graphic design.... Tactile: the feel of the seats, the floor slope, the temperature, the feel of paper, the texture of communion bread, hugs or handshakes, the subwoofer's vibration.... Auditory: volume and frequency levels, clarity, instrumental mix, room noise, congregational sound, stage volume bleed.... Smell & Taste: odors, fragrances, communion elements, breath mints....

2. **Time** — *We offer a moment apart from the regular activity of life*

   Consider the pauses between or within songs, the busyness of a song's arrangement, the pace and flow of the service, reflection, interacting directly with the Lord, responding to the Holy Spirit's guidance in our corporate "worship closet," moments for connect relationally, transitioning....

3. **Enable** — *We address potential hindrances to congregational participation*

   Consider how you communicate expectations, preempt questions, explain service elements, design service structures facilitating worship to unfold, clarify vocabulary, create understanding, model possibilities and passion, teach songs, provide clear melodies, adjust your focal point, provide information, instruct, direct congregational focus, facilitate relational connection....

4. **Invitation** — *We communicate that it's the congregation's turn in a valued, participatory part of the service*

   Consider how you interact, welcome and greet, extend yourself relationally, plainly extend permission for the congregation's turn to engage.

5. **Opportunity** — *We step back and get out of the way*

   Rather than doing everything for the congregation or filling all the time talking or modeling for them, consider how you can communicate that it's the congregation's turn, and then allow them to sing, explain to one another, participate, give, pray, interact, actually express worship to Jesus....

Interacting with God

Not only do we expect that we ourselves worship and that the congregation joins along. Shouldn't we also expect God to join in?

Certainly we should. But I know that I am guilty of designing far too many services so full of activities and expressions of praise that they lack much space for what God might want to do or say other than directly through the people on the platform.

Services are extremely time sensitive. As the one time when nearly all the congregation gathers in the same place, every moment counts.

The tragic temptation is to check off our songs like a "do/done" list and move on immediately to the next service element. The opportunity for connection slips through our fingers.

Like Harry Chapin's old song "Cat's in the Cradle," We put actually dwelling together until some other time; right now we have things to do. Eventually it's too late.

Perhaps we max out our services because we fear that God won't show up. Doesn't it make more sense that our worship times reflect our expectation that God will be there as promised, and so we've reserved moments for prayer, reflection, and responding.

Musically supported pauses for interaction are instrumentals called a "Selah." You'll see the term in some of the corporate worship songs of the Psalms. Creating and performing sets with this kind of spiritual breathing space is another tool in our toolbox for connecting. Usually the congregation needs our help to learn how to approach this time.

Freeing ourselves to take the plunge

In addition to freeing the congregation, several things help allow ourselves to connect during congregational times.

Keep yourself free spiritually. Maintain an attitude of worship throughout the week and avoid entangling sin. Rehearsing with the team and knowing your gear are vital.

But what I find that we most commonly neglect is this: *Preparation.*

Neglecting preparation blocks us from reaching full effectiveness. By not knowing our music well or how to complete tasks efficiently, we fail to give ourselves the mental space needed to connect.

Personal prep is one of the most freeing things we can do.

If you're really serious about connecting, consider memorizing your parts. Perhaps you—like me—dislike the self-discipline required. But it's worth the effort.

I experienced its benefits firsthand as a 13-year-old playing the lead role in a production of *You're A Good Man, Charlie Brown*. The entire cast knew every line—our own and everyone else's—weeks before performances began. This gave us freedom to improvise, developing a comfortable groove with the rest of the cast. We nailed characterization. We could focus on our audience and on each other. Of all the shows in which I performed, that was one of my favorites. Memorization freed us to succeed, and to have a lot of fun doing it.

Consider these three techniques to ease memorization.

1. Simplify your song arrangements. Effectiveness is a higher priority than creating intricate arrangements.

2. Share the responsibilities for playing difficult sections.

3. Start by learning only key places where you anticipate needing to focus on something other than playing.

Doing what is necessary in order to connect personally during our worship sets is one of the most important ways we can become effective. It is part of our sacrifice. It is a great expression of worship.

PAUSE & CONSIDER_____

❑ What additional impact might I have by taking one step to more effectively connect with the congregation and the Lord during our music times together?

7.6 YOUR PIECE OF THE PIE

We live in a golden era when it comes to the availability of musical and technical training. Formal and informal opportunities abound: worship institutions, technical schools, web-based instruction, coaching, workshops, Facebook groups, YouTube.... The difficulty is narrowing down and selecting from all the choices!

I tend to go overboard. I currently subscribe to two websites which provide instrumental instruction and help musicians learn their parts. I use on-line tutorials and watch interviews with musicians who played the original parts on the recordings I like. I download guitar patches and loops. Training websites help me stay fresh on current audio engineering techniques. Two of my adult children use graphic editing software professionally and help keep my skills honed. I connect with people I respect to discover their observations.

Learning helps keep my abilities relevant.

Despite our access to resources, many worship team members fail to take advantage of what's available at their fingertips. Church professionals are often so busy maintaining their programs that they're unwilling to invest time in their own learning.

But everyone doesn't have to be an expert on everything. Share the load. And think of the progress your team could make if they'd each invest just a little time to learn something new.

Knowledge gap

It amazes me how many musicians and technicians have only an elementary understanding of *why* they play what they do or *how* their gear actually works.

Understanding the nuts and bolts of music arranging and technology opens many doors for me both creatively and as a worship facilitator. It provides me the capability to quickly adapt to personnel or equipment surprises.

Have you seen a church team paralyzed when one of their people becomes unavailable and no one can shift roles? Changing song keys may cause a near revolt. Some teams tap only a fraction of their musical potential because they're intimidated by anything other than pounding out chords; they're limited to producing a wall of sonic mush. Many musicians and technicians avoid training others simply because they fear being unable to answer questions.

When we only replicate the dots on the page or the finger movements on a video clip, and have no understanding of why those musical choices are made, it's like limiting a pianist to play with only a single finger. Capable of so much more, we hold ourselves back.

Sometimes we fail to realize the value of our potential.

I first began serving in music ministry at a tricky time. Mainstream worship schools didn't exist. I sought a church music degree from a university where many popular contemporary Christian musicians got their start; classes focused on topics like conducting, hymnology, and music theory. We even had a killer handbell choir. I had to go to a state university to study audio engineering in a professional studio environment.

But even with formal study, much of my practical training came from hands-on experiences traveling as a professional musician. Eventually worship conferences and workshops began to flourish, but in the early days worship musicians and technicians mostly had to figure things out on our own.

Now, even with a plethora of excellent resources, worship schools, and church training programs, many worship team members remain primarily self taught.

There's no good reason for you to function in the dark.

I'd like to cover a couple of foundational concepts that can help you better understand how to address your role. Even though this material is primarily focused toward musicians, the principles can be applied to sound and visual techs as well.

The Pie approach to arranging

I first learned the Pie concept back in the early '80's at a workshop with Glen Kaiser. Dan Wilt taught it at a workshop I attended in the early '90's, and Paul Baloche spelled it out well in his excellent *Worship Team Dynamics* training video. This foundation concept helps musicians realize that adding people to the team means that everyone has to play less.

Otherwise impact falters because the good things being created all blur together into sonic mud.

Basically, the Pie approach to arranging goes like this. Think of all the music notes belonging to a song, the melody, harmonies, rhythm, everything. They are the pie's contents. If you are playing the song all by yourself, you're responsible for the entire pie—all the notes.

If another musician is added, they take their part of the notes. Those notes are not your responsibility anymore, so you don't play them. Add a vocalist, and their slice contains the melody; your slice gets smaller. Add a violin or harmony singer; your slice gets smaller. Every time another musician joins in, your slice is reduced.

Each new instrument adds to the sonic variety of the song. More people grow through serving, more people impact the congregation with their gifts, and the number of connection points between the team and the congregation increases.

You may also have a better chance to replicate the nuances and elements for which you initially selected the song.

With more people dividing the musical parts, you have less to learn and practice. Your focus can become razor sharp.

There are challenges, too. You have to ensure that no one plays another's part unless it's deliberate for effect. Losing one musician throws off the entire arrangement as musicians must shift to fill the gap. Training new musicians may become more complicated. Group rehearsal becomes more important as musicians must blend in tuning, style, and timing. While purchasing song arrangements may bring consistency if your team has the same combination of instruments as the arrangement, that neither allows for flexibility nor trains the musicians to develop creatively.

Some musicians may particularly struggle to share a portion of their piece of the pie if:

- the monitor system does not allow them to hear that someone else is covering a similar part;
- they lack awareness of the need to share a part;
- they are so attached to a part that they find sharing difficult;
- they feel concern that the other musician lacks the needed gear, skill, or awareness to handle a part;
- communicating expectations is poor;
- no one else points out unintentional double coverage.

You may be able to think of other reasons.

The Pie approach also explains why traditionally trained pianists can struggle in a band situation if they rely on learning their part from sheet music. Piano music is usually created by combining all the instrumentation down to a single instrument. This makes using sheet music ineffective for a band arrangement because the pianist plays everyone's parts and clutters the sound. If you remove from the piano part all of the notes covered by other instruments, usually very little remains. Try this experiment and see for yourself!

Many good audio technicians and engineers consider the Pie approach when creating a mix. Because they function as the music producer, they shape the overall balance that the congregation will hear. When multiple instruments are inappropriately doubling parts of the pie, that part usually becomes muddy and disproportionate to the rest of the mix. By minimizing one of those channels in the mix via volume or EQ, that part of the pie can be brought back into balance. The audio engineer provides a safety net for poor arranging and inexperienced musicianship.

Visual technicians (imagery, lyrics, set, projection, lighting) can also consider the Pie approach. They can emphasize whatever needs to be highlighted by directing the congregation's attention appropriately and reducing distractions.

Technicians of any kind can benefit from dividing their responsibilities using their own version of the Pie approach.

More participants means more sacrifice to one's expressive freedom. But it also means increased focus and a shared workload. And when approached correctly, the whole can be so much greater than the sum of its parts.

PAUSE & CONSIDER

❑ How can my willingness to share my piece of the pie allow me to increase my impact?

7.7 YOUR PLACE IN THE SONIC FIELD

Reducing music responsibilities according to the Pie approach can remove sonic mud by allowing each musician to impact a song.

But what if the musicians don't really understand musical roles in the first place? Other than perhaps the octave they play in, they may not be sure what part to keep and what part to share.

Most of us initially approach music intuitively according to our preferences. Although formal study provides cognitive awareness, many of us would prefer visiting the dentist. The worship teams I work with find that understanding a few foundational concepts helps them to create more effective parts *and* be better team members. You may find this, too.

A musical tapestry

Considering creation's incredible variety, Jesus seems to like how unique parts blend together into a unified whole. The diversity of human cultural expression reflects this, too.

Part of our task when preparing contemporary music is weaving together individual musicians, technicians, and a room full of people.

No one musical style is innately *the* most aesthetically pleasing to God. Although some forms seem more effective for different groups of people, because human culture changes, we are wise to remain open as God leads us into fresh ways of worshiping Him.

Songs and other art forms used by the Church over the centuries are like standing stones reminding us of the Lord's faithfulness, His nature, His handiwork, and His interaction with us. New songs written throughout the Church worldwide reflect the current movements of God. We select from a richly diverse palette!

The Bible says in Ephesians 5:19-20:

"Speak to one another with psalms, hymns, and spiritual songs. Sing and make music in your heart to the Lord, always giving thanks to God the Father for everything, in the name of our Lord Jesus Christ. Submit to one another out of reverence for Christ."

Colossians 3:16 words it a bit differently:

"Let the word of Christ dwell in you richly as you teach and admonish one another with all wisdom, and as you sing psalms, hymns, and spiritual songs with gratitude in your hearts to God."

See the variety? Poetic songs share what it means to walk with Him. Traditional songs of the Church declare His truths. Fresh and intimate songs emotionally express the Bride's heart to the Groom— all sung with thanksgiving that overflows from walking with Him.

There's really something for everyone.

PAUSE & CONSIDER_____

❑ How can I include people who connect with the Lord through different songs and styles than those I find meaningful?

8 musical roles in a song

Regardless of musical style and the specific instruments being used, several key musical concepts increases impact.

Think of an orchestra—a stage full of instruments capable of making an incredible wall of sound. But even without a sound board and amplification, with skillful arrangement a single flute can stand out distinctly. Or an oboe, or a cello, or a viola, or a trombone....

Musicians should know their specific role in a song. Otherwise they often simply play away, regardless of their effect upon what the other musicians do. It makes sense that our impact increases when we know how our role fits with the rest of what the team plays.

Sometimes worship leaders and team directors don't help.

Being a worship leader is not necessarily a highly challenging role musically. We may simply sing the melody and hammer out chords. This frees us to focus on other important aspects of the role like leading the team and interacting with the congregation.

> *When our musical role feels less demanding, we may assume that other musicians* **have an equally easy time handling** *their own musical roles. This is not necessarily true.*

Many times, worship team members have never learned exactly what musical function their part plays within the overall structure of the rest of the team. This lack of knowledge results in a jumbled musical mess doing little to engage the congregation.

Each musician serving in a contemporary church band performs at least one of these eight primary musical roles in a song.

1. **Melody** — This is the primary tune of the song - you sing along with it. It's what you hum it to someone when you're trying to help them remember the tune. It's usually sung by the lead vocalist and most of the congregation.

2. **Harmony** — These lines usually move in parallel or opposite direction with the melody. Harmonies may be vocal or instrumental. They're usually continual in hymn and gospel music styles. *Contemporary music often reserves harmonies for key places in the song.*

3. **Groove** — This is the primary rhythm of the song. It's what

you clap along with or tap your feet to. Most instruments usually need to synch to those establishing the groove.

4. **Primary Instrument** — This is the single instrument around which the other instruments form their parts. Usually, unless the song is a cappella (vocals only), this is the one instrument necessary to play the song. *There should only be one primary instrument at any given moment.*

5. **Counter-Melody** — This is a melody that isn't the primary vocal line. It could be a fill between lines of the song, a lead, a hook, or a descant. Counter melodies are usually shorter than the melody, and they usually should not cover up the melody.

6. **Texture** — Often played by a keyboard pad or reverb/delayed guitar, this part fills in the sonic spectrum underneath the other instruments like glue to support and bring the other parts together.

7. **Color** — These parts add touches of accents to give the song character or highlight something important in the lyrics or other song roles. *When overdone, it loses impact.*

8. **Silence** — This is when a musician waits without playing until the opportune moment to reenter the song and have special impact. Think of the cymbal player waiting for the song's crescendo. It's probably the most challenging role of all!

Knowing your role frees you from wasting focus on extraneous parts. Even if you exchange roles with another musician at a given point in a song, keeping to one role at a time declutters the song's musical texture. It helps you more significantly impact the worship expression that your team creates.

PAUSE & CONSIDER_____

❑ How does recognizing my primary musical role impact my role?

234

7.8 BUILDING CONTRAST

Sometimes instrument combinations, even if playing completely different roles, still produce sonic mud. This effect is sometimes referred to a creating the dreaded "wall of sound."

Good questions we may ask ourselves to address this include:

- "How can I stand out without burying someone else?"

- "How do I know *when* to stand out?"

- "How do I know *who* should stand out in this song?"

- "What can I add to make the song interesting?"

- "How can I simplify my part to keep it distinct and sharpen its impact?"

These can be challenging questions. Communication with the worship leader and team members during practices and rehearsals help us know the song's direction and feel. We also have to know when to blend, and when to be distinct.

Few of us like musical mud.

Although the sound technician can help distinguish or blend instruments by adjusting volume levels, equalization, gates, compression, delay, and reverb, the musicians themselves have the greatest capability to create contrast between parts so that each person can have maximum musical impact and expression. This ability is one of the characteristics that distinguishes a quality musician.

The key is arranging each instrument within the appropriate area of the sonic field. Properly combining instruments greatly simplifies the sound tech's job at the mixer—it's all "Get It Right At The Source" Arranging 101.

The following three main considerations help each instrument find its unique place in the overall musical texture of a song.

1. **Rhythmic Domain** - A song's groove provides the rhythm upon which the primary instrument and the melody are hung. Rhythm instruments usually include the drums/percussion, bass, and rhythm guitar or piano/keys. Instruments can distinguish themselves by focusing on whole, quarter, or eighth notes, diamonds, accents, backbeats/offbeats, etc. Generally all instruments need to be in synch with the song's groove, even when playing different parts of it.

   A drum set is a good micro-example of different instruments working together in the rhythmic domain. The kick plays the 1, 3, and 4 1/2. The high hat plays sixteenths. The snare plays quarters. The toms come in on the turnaround between lines. The cymbals add color and emphasis as needed. Each drum plays distinctly different note lengths, but together they create a whole.

2. **Pitch & Timbre Domain** - Each instrument plays in a specific octave range and has its own unique timbre (tone), possibly modified by effects. These factors can be used to help instruments blend or to make them stand out.

   Two guitars provide a good example of using pitch and timbre to create sonic separation. One guitar plays lower on the neck in a different octave than the second guitar, which stays higher up. One guitar uses a full sound, the second plays with a thinner and brighter tone to cut through. A third guitar stays lower, but only plays the two lowest strings and uses distortion to sound different sonically. (Additionally they could use the rhythmic domain by the lower guitar strumming 16ths, the 2-stringing guitar playing diamonds— whole notes—and the higher guitar playing diamonds or arpeggiated notes.)

3. **Melodic Domain** - This refers to more than the part of the song you sing or hum along to (the primary melody). It considers harmonies, counter-melodies, turnarounds, color, fills, leads, and pads. Melody is king. All other instruments should be spaced around the melody to enable it to be clear and strong. Ask yourself, is the melody going up or down here, and should I move parallel, opposite, or in some other way in relationship to it?"

   For example, the background vocals could all sing harmonies which move in parallel to the lead vocal singing melody, with a bass singer singing notes moving opposite the direction of the melody. A background choir could do "ah" common tones without moving with the melody. An additional vocal could sing a descant or an alternative melody (perhaps the bridge line) as the lead vocal sings the chorus melody. And a lead guitar plays its own melody as a hook during the turnaround before the verses and during the exit.

If all instruments match one another in all three of these domains, they'll be pretty indistinguishable (if you play well). Matching in two domains still tends to lack clarity, though there's a better chance each instrument may have some impact. Instruments with a unique place in all three domain areas have the most distinguishable character and much greater effect on the song.

The easy way out is to ignore the other instruments and hope the sound technicians fix things in the mix. They can sweep EQ to bring out an instrument's sweet spot, and create frequency holes in an instrument's channel so that those frequencies are more easily heard from other instruments. They can use reverb or delay to make parts less distinct or present. Or they could simply reduce a competing instrument in the mix.

While these Band-Aids can help (they're great for mixing and mastering recordings), great musicianship is superior.

There's a good reason why of the 64 times that the word "skill" is found in the Bible, many are used in the context of honoring God in the temple.

The excellence with which we create our offerings to the Lord reflects how we value our relationship with Him. He is worthy of our best effort.

By knowing your musical role and creating parts that help you stand out, you can offer up your own distinct expression that enriches the musical texture. It helps create an inviting opportunity for the team and congregation to engage with the Lord together. It enables your expression to make a musical difference and give voice to the praise.

PAUSE & CONSIDER_____

❑ How can I bring my own creative thumbprint to my role on the music team and better express worship?

7. 9 EMBRACING UNIQUENESS

Most people serving in music ministry care that what they do matters. You probably share many of these values.

- Our work makes a difference.

- We invest ourselves to develop skill, acquire knowledge, and develop presentation.

- We learn from the thoughts and life lessons experienced by others.

- We embrace the gift/ministry mix He invested into us. We want to be more.

- We acknowledge that authenticity requires continual growth.

- We realize that our internal growth must outrace the outward person we present ourselves to be.

Even the secular world recognizes that appearance without substance eventually crashes. The ancient Greeks called this concept "Hubris." King Solomon declared in Proverbs 16:18 that such an attitude is followed by destruction.

I like Shakespeare's depiction of the "shallow performer" in his play *Macbeth*.

"Life's but a walking shadow, a poor player

That struts and frets his hour upon the stage,
And then is heard no more. It is a tale
Told by an idiot, full of sound and fury,
Signifying nothing." [23]

Ouch! That last bit really strikes me as both a reprimand and a warning.

"It is a tale told by an idiot, full of sound and fury, signifying nothing."

Even with good values, many of us struggle with the slow road that transformation seems to require. I know my impatience rises!

When we try to fast-track the path, we skip transformation. There's no such thing as "virtual" growth.

People want to see what's real in us.

Have you ever found yourself scramble to fill 12 seconds of awkward silence by saying something that you've heard but really haven't learned the full truth of for yourself?

I have. But I'm sure we'd both rather speak from an overflow of what the Lord is teaching us, the stuff we've paid dearly to embed into our lives. Real depth.

Of course, doing that assumes we remain teachable and use good measuring sticks.

It's easy to mistake head knowledge for growth. But, just as depicted by the Tree of Life and the Tree of Knowledge in Eden's garden, knowledge in itself will not birth kingdom-building fruit. Rather than allow us to live off of lessons from days gone by, God provides experiences and situations enabling us to address the one or two new things He knows we need to learn right now.

Shortcuts to growth

Instead, we can be tempted to seek a short cut to growth.

---

[23] Macbeth, Act 5, scene 5, lines 16—27.

So we learn new techniques, buy new gear, squeeze into skinnier jeans, pack our set lists with popular tunes, memorize the catch phrases of the day. But as cool and enticing as they may be, these things supply no path to real spiritual growth.

There is one common growth catalyst.

Many of the people who I respect for their deep pools of maturity and wisdom have experienced something in common: extreme personal loss or pain. Tragedy can bring great growth.

I immediately think of Nancy. Throughout the 12 years I served with her, I cannot recall ever hearing her complain about her wheelchair, the loss of mobility, disappointment from relying upon others who let her down, or the daily pain as her disease irreversibly transforms her body's muscles and soft tissue into solid bone. Yet she amazes and challenges me. She is humble. She fiercely captures every moment. She remains one of the most positive and productive people I've ever met. She has depth I cannot begin to understand.

Even so, I dare not ask for her situation! I couldn't handle it.

I do *not* suggest that all tragedy is a person's fault. Nancy's certainly isn't. I simply suggest that from the outside looking in, some of us, like Nancy, have especially difficult routes bearing deep fruit.

PAUSE & CONSIDER

❏ How has the terrible difficulty of a lesson I have learned made that lesson all the more invaluable?

Although God may redeem suffering or struggle into a growth step—turning straw into gold—it's not a short cut we should create on our own. If it does come, we should simply follow Nancy's example and respond with a faithful attitude conducive to growth.

Growth is challenging enough on its own. Why make it harder?

Expecting to obtain growth by taking a short cut is—looking for the best word—*stupid*. Consider scriptural examples of the price people paid for trying an easier way. Sampson. Jacob. Moses. David.

The Children of Israel on the way to and entering the promised land. Yes, lessons were learned, but the cost was tragic, often leaving a string of bodies in its wake, which generally could have been avoided had they not followed their own inclination in the first place.

The list of my own faulty personal attempts is embarrassingly long. Yours probably contains at least a few items.

Here's the single best, fastest, most direct route to growth and impact: Stay on the path that the Lord designed for you.

Who could possibly understand each of us better than Creator God? He designs a custom-built curriculum for each of us to grow with the Holy Spirit's guidance to transform into something incredibly special, and He invests in each of us a unique gift package through which we each can minister and impact others.

I may not understand His choices, but I'm learning to trust His design. You can, too. Joyfully embrace the transformation that He offers you through serving. Tap into your potential by investing every part of your being—heart, mind, body, will, skills, resources, relationships—everything that makes up your deepest identity.

God made each person singularly, *peculiarly* unique. Heart, mind, soul, experiences, relationships, abilities... no one in all creation may approach Him—worship Him—like you. No one can counterfeit your exact consequence or impact upon the world. No one can fill your place in the Bride. No one can replicate the best that you can be.

You are irreplaceable.

ABOUT TIMOTHY J MILLER

I help church professionals, leaders, and worship-arts volunteers to develop more impact. Some of my tools for accomplishing this include writing, teaching, and coaching.

I said, "Yes" to Jesus in 1970. Five years later I began serving through music. While I've grown up, learned, lived, worked, married, and raised my family mostly in Illinois, Indiana, and Michigan, my wife and I now live in Sarasota, FL. We don't miss snow.

What matters to me most is that after you and I connect, you can continue on better equipped to experience the Lord. Through our encounter, I want you to enjoy Him more. Your growth glorifies Him and brings Him pleasure, too.

The crowns we'll both place at His feet in eternity will grow.

And that thought brings me joy. Thank you!

ADDITIONAL RESOURCES

I wrestle with adequately conveying how important it is that you can apply concepts from this book to your own life and ministry. Your feedback is so helpful!

Yesterday I received a phone call from someone who wanted to share how something I said 25 years ago has helped shape how they walk under authority, including their willingness to trust the Lord. It seemed such a simple concept at the time. But it grew profoundly. That's how the Lord often works. And it is so exciting when we realize what His hand was doing and that we played a part.

I don't know how confident you feel to use this material as you step forward on your own or go through this with your team. You are the only one who can determine that.

But what if you could have me available to walk with you through the whole process? How would that boost your confidence level? That could be exciting!

That's why I create Thinking Partner groups and provide growth coaching. Collaborating is so rewarding, and there's nothing like being a resource to growth. At least for me, it seems that many of us thrive best when we have a partner.

I look forward to connecting with you as we each experience God's MORE for our lives!   —*Tim*

Made in the USA
Middletown, DE
27 May 2019